EVEN
AFTER
EVERYTHING

EVEN
AFTER
EVERYTHING

The Spiritual Practice of Knowing the Risks
and Loving Anyway

Stephanie Duncan Smith

CONVERGENT

NEW YORK

Published in the United States by Convergent Books, an imprint of Random House, a division of Penguin Random House LLC, New York.

CONVERGENT BOOKS is a registered trademark and the Convergent colophon is a trademark of Penguin Random House LLC.

Library of Congress Cataloging-in-Publication Data
Names: Duncan Smith, Stephanie, author.
Title: Even after everything / Stephanie Duncan Smith.
Description: First edition. | New York, NY: Convergent, 2024.
Identifiers: LCCN 2024034018 (print) | LCCN 2024034019 (ebook) |
ISBN 9780593727751 (hardcover) | ISBN 9780593727768 (ebook)
Subjects: LCSH: Church year. | Church calendar. |
Promises—Biblical teaching.
Classification: LCC BV30 .D77 2024 (print) | LCC BV30 (ebook) |
DDC 263/.9—dc23/eng/20240805
LC record available at https://lccn.loc.gov/2024034018
LC ebook record available at https://lccn.loc.gov/2024034019

Printed in the United States of America on acid-free paper

convergentbooks.com

2 4 6 8 9 7 5 3 1

First Edition

Book design by Caroline Cunningham

We are radically accompanied.
—WENDY WRIGHT, *The Vigil*

To Quinn and Soren:

May you tesser well, in the trust that you

are always "radically accompanied."

And to all who have dared to open themselves

to love and loving again.

CONTENTS

WHERE WE BEGIN

When I think of the liturgical year, I think of a color wheel—expressive of the full range of human emotion. Advent anticipation, Lenten lament, Holy Saturday anguish, and Easter joy are familiar to us, because they are all shades of the human experience. Even the liturgical colors express these emotions implicitly, moving through penitential purples, celebratory white and golds, fire red of Pentecost, the green of Ordinary Time's growing season.

The only problem is that these larger seasons and their particular emotional color rarely line up with the color and emotion of our personal moment. This is the problem with which this work contends.

I have written the book you now hold in your hands over the course of four pregnancies.

After a decade of chosen childlessness with my husband, I warmed to the wonder of my first pregnancy during Advent, only to lose this pregnancy on the winter solstice's longest night, just as the world readied to celebrate its most historic birth on Christmas.

My second pregnancy unfolded in unsettling parallel to the global pandemic, and I gave birth to our daughter nearly one year to the day after our first loss. Her birthday marked the peak of pandemic deaths in our city to date at the time. It was also Advent's week of joy.

My third pregnancy ended too soon—strangely, on what should have been the midsummer birthday of our first. This day held both the ghost of what should have been, and the ghost of what should never have been. I miscarried the same day we said goodbye to the family dog, and I had to explain death to my eighteen-month-old again and again, just when I understood it the least.

And my fourth brought us our son—our gentle giant newborn who, as I write this, sleeps on my chest.

How to make sense of such deep griefs, great joys, and unsettling in-betweens? Writing helped, so that's what I did. I wrote through the changing of the clocks bringing daylight saving darkness in the fall, through the candlelit weeks of Advent, then as the last of the Christmas trees were taken out to the curb. I wrote through the turning of the seasons—first frosts, first sightings of green, the last of the leaves falling like embers. I wrote through the carpal tunnel of postpartum wrists, thumbs on my phone in dark mode during midnight feedings. I wrote from our row house front porch on sweltering summer nights watching the baby monitor.

Through it all, I was writing into the problem of dissonance. Once, I sat down with a Sharpie and a pack of multicolored sticky notes, and I wrote it out as an act of witness. On one color, I wrote out the seasons of the Christian calendar, which is the way I am accustomed to keeping time in the liturgical tradition. I lined them up on the rug on the floor. On another color, I wrote out the timeline of personal events—which for me were defined by the warping effect of pandemic time and the acuteness of time as experienced through pregnancy trimesters. I stacked this color—robin's-egg blue—on top of the first, a quiet lilac.

There on the rug, these timelines braided together in color, a new picture emerged. I found that as I stacked these personal events on top of the seasons of the liturgical year, they told a wholly new story, their interconnections at turns deeply painful, beautiful, and surprising.

I imagine you could say the same.

If you had your own color timeline, I imagine your own personal moments—when overlaid with the rhythms of life, death, and resurrection as the liturgical year cycles through again and again—would tell quite a story.

Life, death, and rebirth are the essential rhythms of the natural world, the sacred year, and the human experience. Sometimes our personal moments converge with these natural and sacred seasons in profound, meaning-rich ways. And sometimes they clash with unbearable disparity. If time is a color wheel, every new day turns it like a kaleidoscope, so that every new day, the view changes.

This book is an exploration in the dizzying problem of dissonance—what happens when our human moment bitterly juxtaposes the sacred season and its proclaimed hope, and what this might mean for us. There is no denying the dissonance. Yet there is also no denying that the story the sacred year reflects—of God becoming one of us—mirrors every facet of the human experience. From Advent to Ordinary Time, the liturgical year cycles through deeply human themes of love, risk, great joy, dark nights, uncertain in-betweens, and new beginnings. I began to read this mirroring as divine empathy, which is the very spirit of intent behind the liturgical tradition to begin with, as the church through the centuries has foraged for ways to make sense of God-with-us in our time. And in this empathy, I began to find the consolation that we are seen and may even be steadied by a love that stays with us through it all.

Each chapter in this book braids a personal moment with the larger liturgical moment, at turns reckoning with and reflecting how God meets us in our here and now, for whatever it holds. I trust you have your own griefs, joys, and unsettled in-betweens, just as you have your own problem of dissonance. The particulars may look different—mine are the experience of pregnancy and pregnancy loss, as well as the world-shaping pandemic, which for some may feel far removed now years later. But in our shared search for steadiness, I have come to believe the liturgical year can become both an empathizing mirror as well as an anchoring force.

There are varied expressions of the Christian year across traditions, but the shared arc is its tracing of the major events in the life of Christ through our calendar today, inviting us into the practice of sacred time and its ultimate hope of life after death, even in and against the tragedies of mortal time. The liturgical year follows seven primary movements through Christ's life as it converges with ours:

Advent is a season of waiting found in the four weeks prior to Christ's birth and "coming" on Christmas. It is a season of expectation, with room for both joyful anticipation as well as longing punctuated by lament as we recall Israel's cries for a savior to come and deliver just as the prophets had promised.

Christmas, of course, commemorates the birth of Christ, as both a feast day and a traditional celebration of twelve days. It is a season of wonder and joy, as we marvel at the mystery of the

Incarnation and the ancient promises fulfilled in this newborn God who bears a new age with him.

Epiphany is the feast day observed after Christmas, celebrating the Magi's star-led journey to worship the Christ child. The weeks following leading up to Lent are a bridge of Ordinary Time often referred to as the "season of light," signifying the light of the world coming not just for Israel but for all people. This season observes the revelations of Christ turning water to wine, his baptism, and the beginning of his public ministry as he is called into the work of God.

Lent is the season of forty days—minus Sundays, which are always feast days—carrying us from Ash Wednesday to Easter. Lent follows the narrative of Christ's temptation in the wilderness and his journey toward the cross, inviting us into a season of reckoning with our mortality, and the sins and suffering of our own and of the world's, in the spirit of preparation to receive Christ's gift for the life of the world.

Holy Week is the bridge between Lent and Easter, remembering the Passion Week of Christ. It begins with Palm Sunday and Jesus' triumphal entry into Jerusalem, and observes the Last Supper given on Maundy Thursday, the crucifixion on Good Friday, and the unsettling silence of Holy Saturday.

Easter is the feast day of all feast days, the central celebration of the Christian faith, as it bears the news that Christ has risen. Eastertide is the fifty-day season of celebration that follows, giving the church time to absorb the astonishing reality of the resurrection. Traditionally, Eastertide concludes on Pentecost, the feast day observing the outpouring of the Spirit on God's people.

And finally, *Ordinary Time* spans the summer and early autumn months until the circle begins anew with another Advent. The word "ordinary" stems from the word "ordinal," meaning simply the counted days, or the numbered Sundays, that compose this season, which is the lengthiest of them all. But it also speaks to the promise that God is with us in our ordinary lives, not just the high holidays. It is a season of growth, practice, and transformation, as the church is called to live into its mission.

"Liturgy" means simply the work of the people. And if the liturgy is the work of the people, it is first the work of a life. It is the work of finding new patterns in the oldest human story. It is the work of keeping time by tracing the life of Christ through the circle of the year, as well as the labor of confronting the dissonance between our human experience and the seasons of sacred time. Yet this dissonance, as I have found, can also be a place of divine encounter, as God becomes one of us and meets us in the full-color spectrum of the human experience. As the color wheel turns, every human situation is brought into conversation with a sacred season, creating an encounter with God that is wholly unique to us in our present moment.

Liturgical time is not something fixed, far removed, or a dusty custom from long ago. Rather, the practice of keeping liturgical time yields a lived narrative that is ancient, present, and ever new. It is ancient, in that it tells the oldest story known to humankind. It is present, in that this ancient story converges with the story of our lived experience right now. And it is ever new: as these two stories come together in dynamic conversation—an eye-to-eye encounter with the God who became one of us.

Neither is it a red-roped exclusive tradition, reserved for certain types of people who happen to resonate with "high church" expressions. Because the essential rhythms of life, death, and rebirth belong to all of us, and it is only human practice to try and find meaning in this cycle of things.

And so this book is for anyone questioning how to stay steady in the midst of the unresolved. It's for anyone who has ever felt unseen by the joy of a season, or of others, that is so far removed from their current experience. It's for anyone who is worn out by the pressures and imperatives to bounce back or power through, and still, who longs to locate whatever muscles can sustain them through unsettling times.

The book, as you now receive it here, has been written, set in ink. But the encounter of human moment with sacred season is a story I will be living my entire life. Through the cycling of the seasons and the turning color wheel of a life, this story will take on new layers, new meaning, and—if I'm paying attention—new depths of divine encounter. My hope is that it will do the same for you.

EVEN
AFTER
EVERYTHING

1

SEARCHING FOR STEADINESS

Ordinary Time

I AM the constant
With You in every variable of the unknown

Peace is the centre of the atom, the core
Of quiet within the storm. . . .
The primal image: God within the heart.

       MADELEINE L'ENGLE, *The Weather of the Heart*

When I first plugged the dates into the due date estimator online, I let out a gasp of surprise when I saw the date it gave me: December 25. Not just because it was Christmas Day, but also because it meant this baby would be born a year nearly to the day that we lost our first.

That gasp held the predicament that has haunted all of humankind from the beginning: Ultimately, if this—if anything—is a love story, it is also a risk story. To open ourselves to love is to expose ourselves to the Great Asterisk that renders every love—large or small, person or passion—vulnerable to the terrible risks of loss. Love and loss are always closer than we'd care to confess. The line between the two is thin as the rim of a coin, and, as if tossed into the air, ever shimmering.

And I felt more exposed than ever. Just months after losing our first pregnancy and in the first trimester of this new pregnancy, I found myself sitting half naked and alone in an exam room waiting for an ultrasound after the handheld Doppler couldn't find the heartbeat.

I had heard those words before—"we can't find the heartbeat"— and my panic swelled now like the high tide as my body remembered. Being told that death has happened inside of you while you are still alive is not something the body ever forgets. A shock like that gets locked inside muscle memory for a lifetime, and it was coming roaring back for me now.

"It's still early," the nurse, Maggie, had told me as she left the room. "The Doppler doesn't pick up everything this early along. We'll get you in there, hon." Maggie was the one I often talked to when I called with my many questions. She always called me hon, in the Middle Tennessee accent we would come to know so well during the years we spent in Knoxville for my husband's doctoral program.

It was early summer, the first summer after the pandemic had been declared. Just months before, in March, two biological events in microscopic scale began in parallel, and they would change my life forever in dramatically different ways. Particles. Cells. The smallest measurable matter began gathering force. One would culminate, or so we hoped, in the birth of our child, a person we had not yet met but to whom we would belong forever. The other would result in a pandemic causing six million worldwide deaths and untold tragedies, all brought about by something so small we couldn't see, forever splicing the lives of survivors into the kind of before-and-after no one ever asked for.

It was astonishing to consider how something so small, smaller than the period at the end of a sentence, could loom so large in consequence for our lives. And the very same could be said about this new life growing inside of me. After my pregnancy was confirmed, my husband, Zach, and I moved through each week with conflicting emotions: hope that my body's hormones and this baby's cells would keep multiplying toward life, and paralyzing fear as we watched case counts and deaths in their exponential climb.

We were keenly aware that this pregnancy right on the heels of our first loss was still early, still intensely vulnerable. So when the pink parallel lines revealed themselves, I had known this could be the beginning, or the beginning of the end. There was joy, but it was joy of the brittle sort, if only because I didn't know if I could trust it yet.

And so my pregnancy became the experience of clashing polarities: How can you possibly hold in tension the hope that radical love inspires against life's terrible risks? How can you live every day facing down the probability factors of life or death? Every day, I screened for symptoms—was that a tickle in my throat? Was I breathing okay? Every cough, a question I dared not answer. Every time I went to the bathroom, I feared blood, even as I looked for signs of life—cravings for Pink Lady apples and Earl Grey, gagging every time I brushed my teeth. Every day I hoped, and I feared my hope.

For some women pregnancy is a state of wonder. I was one of them, for a time. For others it is a state of fight, flight, or freeze, except you can't fight what you can't control. Not really. And you can't fly from your own body. So mostly you freeze, in a suspension of fear, powerlessness, anxious unknown. The possibility of loss was a constant presence, quietly shadowing my every move.

The physical markers of threat didn't help, either. When I arrived at the clinic that morning for what was a routine first-trimester checkup, I was wearing a mask that I had affixed in the car before entering. Medical staff in their N95s intercepted me at the door for a temperature check and screening questions. I pumped hand sanitizer on my way to the elevators, even though I had gloves on, and let another woman go first since we couldn't stay six feet apart in the elevator. These were the days the mere sight of nostrils could send me into an anxiety attack. I had hardly left my house in two months, working from home, getting groceries delivered. Doing so now felt precarious, like walking headlong into a minefield.

The angel told Mary, "Do not fear." But now—as I pressed oily palm prints into the exam table paper—my system was flooded with it. It became an unholy baptism, my every nerve ending immersed in sweat-beaded cortisol and held under.

Minutes bled into tens, twenty, more. I could feel myself spiraling. I scanned the room for a still point, something I could focus on to hold me steady, the way focusing on a doorknob or light switch helps me keep my balance in a yoga pose. Not the clock. Not my phone. This was no time for scrolling.

But even as I scrambled for steadiness, the tensions within charged and sparked like signal fires on some forgotten shore. And the silence only fanned their flames. How was I to make sense of the wonder of moving through my first trimester during Advent, as I had just months earlier, only to lose my pregnancy the week before the world would celebrate its most historic birth?

Was it brave or simply reckless to try for life while the deadliest global health crisis in modern memory rapidly gathered force? Was it love or a radical failure of care to bring a child into such a world? In a global moment in which a "positive" test result could mean either the best news or the worst scenario, were Zach and I supposed to feel thrilled or terrified in the face of two pink lines?

And how, in the tension familiar to all who love, could a love so full, so fierce, render us so vulnerable, so afraid, so helpless to protect this little one from harm?

These were the variables. Where was the constant?

I closed my eyes in a desperate search for center. There was nothing for me to do except keep breathing, so that's what I did there on the exam table, and the rhythm slowly took the shape of an improvised breath prayer I have kept with me ever since:

Deep inhale: *I AM*

Long exhale: *With Us*

Again, again, again. "I AM," the name God revealed of God-self. "With Us," the name of God-born-human, a promise of presence in every moment. This one, too. The "us" was important to me. Because even now, as I sat alone on the exam table, I prayed to God there were still two of us.

If ever I was in a liminal space, it was now.

Liminality is derived from the Latin word *limen,* meaning "threshold," and anthropologists have coded liminal spaces as the transition between the before and after of a defining rite of passage. For the rest of us, it may be defined more simply as living in the ellipses—the unsettled in-between where there are no maps. Liminality is a place where contingencies and counterfactuals haunt every hope. On such a quaking threshold, our illusions of control are shaken loose. The certainties of centuries are shattered, as poet Janet Kalven writes.[1] Liminality can be a profoundly disempowering place to find oneself.

Certainly, there were no maps here. Zach and I were living between the pain of pregnancy loss and the hope of new life on its way. Between the loss of prepandemic normalcy and the uncharted unknowns of whatever the future would become. Between a missing heartbeat and an ultrasound that may or may not prove all was well. Between so many shades of before and after.

The I AM is With Us. In this liminal moment, with all its shimmering variables, it was the truest thing I knew.

The I AM is With Us. I was teaching my body to remember. I was expanding my rib cage to take in so solid a truth, trying to release my tension as I exhaled. Trying to let this promise steady me even as I spiraled.

Finally, the door latch clicked, and I opened my eyes. "We're ready for you now," Maggie said, eyes smiling, though I could not see her face behind her mask. I squinted at the clock. I'd been waiting alone for forty-five minutes.

Just minutes later, I was in a blue gown again, looking up at a bright profile of a ten-week-old baby on a dark screen, mercifully moving in a spirited swim. The *whoosh-whoosh* of a steady heartbeat filled the room.

"There we are!" the doctor said, one of a rotating staff I had not met before. "Here, look—" She pointed at the screen. "Your placenta is growing in the anterior position, at the front of your stomach, which is why the Doppler probably couldn't pick up the heartbeat. It creates a sort of buffer."

"Is that a problem?" I asked.

"Oh no," she said, busying herself clacking into the keyboard. "Placentas can situate front, back, side. Perfectly normal."

"So," I said. "So this is not a high-risk pregnancy?" I was convinced this was too easy. Something must be wrong.

The doctor stopped typing and turned toward me. "This is not a high-risk pregnancy. This is a healthy pregnancy. It's always one day at a time, but right now, you and your baby are doing great. There is no cause for concern."

It was the whiplash of relief that broke me when I made it to the privacy of my car. I was holding a trio of ultrasound photos to take home to Zach, three new images at which to marvel, to post up on our fridge. Bent over my steering wheel, I was shaken by the almost, by the been-here-before, by the grace of being found okay for now—God-with-us, *us,* after all.

There's a young adult novel by Gary Schmidt called *Okay for Now* about a kid who finds himself in the in-between. The title phrase is inspired by a James Audubon oil painting of a snowy heron, standing regal and resolute in the riverbank foreground, though the frame also holds a hunter who can be seen advancing from a distance.

Hope is like the snowy heron—a wild thing hiding in the bush, heart pounding in the calm before the choice: fight, flight, or freeze. White plumed and majestic, stepping forward and not back, "beak pointed out to the world,"[2] even against a man advancing with a gun. Safety and threat locked in silent face-off. Never has there been so much swarming adrenaline in a still frame. It is a dare: *Try me.*

When fear menaces our hope, when we have no knowledge or control over what happens next, all we have is the now. Frame by frame. Breath by breath. Beat by beat.

I AM With Us. Each moment, pulling for the wild thing of hope.

Carrying any kind of hope after your hope has died is like this. Today, in the frame of this moment, okay for now. I broke in my car because I knew this is where I lived now: in the space between loss and hope of new life, in the liminality between the world we once knew and whatever it would become in the aftermath of a world-tilting pandemic.

And I'd be living here awhile yet, with many months of pregnancy and who knew how many months of pandemic uncertainty ahead of me.

These were the variables. Where was the constant?

I was going to have to figure out how to keep hope alive in a world of very real high risks. I was going to have to figure out how to hold steady in the "okay for now."

Such is the human predicament: We live in mortal time, and for all the depth of any love, the inevitability and tragedy of mortal time is death. We live our lives in the "okay for now" between the first breath and the last, the liminal state before the end. Whether you're waiting for medical test results, the exhale of making it financially through the month, the nervous system to settle, the chronic pain to stop hurting so chronically, we all know what it's like to be the white heron. "Okay for now" is a place we have all lived, and it is a conflicted place for any of us.

Death, like the hunter, challenges us openly: *Is any love really worth the risk, given the end?* The risks are great. Too great, death claims, to even try. Its most overt argument: *Love is nothing but a setup for loss.*

Mortal time is heavy, bearing the weight of infinite vectors and variants—some bright and beautiful, some unbearable. Mortal time is freighted with love, yes, but also loss and liminality, and so the heart is kept in constant calculus:

Between playing it safe and going all in, heart first.

Between hoping for the best and fearing the worst.

Between saying yes to the life fully lived and yes to what could just as easily be our undoing.

Between every vaulted high and whiplash low, every new-beginning joy and last-rites sorrow, and every shade of before and after.

What can we do but make our choices, take our chances, stake our love against the risk-riddled multiverse of all the ways it could go wrong? The clash of hope against high-risk can be crazy making for anyone. It's no wonder we get twitchy in the here and now. It's enough to make anyone spiral.

And yet, there is a story running counter to the spiral, as well as a long, centuries-old tradition of practicing this story to steady us in our own story. The church calendar, as formed across time and various Christian expressions, follows the life of Christ in distinct seasonal movements, inviting us into the practice of keeping what is often called sacred time.

From the beginning in Advent through the end of its cycle in Ordinary Time, the liturgical year tells a story that mirrors this drama of the human experience: the wonder of new life, the unknowing of the in-between, the death of hope, living hell, and the astonishment of new beginnings. Much like our lives, sacred time is studded with the striking polarities of love, loss, and liminality. This is a story that holds ashes and ascension, silent nights and bitter betrayals, bread and wine and burial spices, weddings and God in human voice crying, *Why?*

The one thing this story will not do is skim the surface. This story does not skip tracks, nor look away when the scene gets intense. Rather, the range of the liturgical story becomes for us one of its greatest gifts, expressing the radical empathy of God *with us* in every human moment—the *I AM* incarnate in our joy, fear, sorrow, and surprise. God in every gradient of the color wheel that composes a life.

The liturgical story also gives us the great hope of our future with God. Mortal time is a closed circuit, the story of all things leading six feet into the low, full stop. Yet through the Incarnation, Jesus entered into the tragedy of mortal time so he might lead us into the story of all things made new. Sacred time tells the subversive story of hope in which every requiem will ultimately give way to resurrection, and this hope can be a profoundly steadying force amid the traumas and terrors of our here and now.

There is a long tradition of understanding liturgical time as a cycle, and its calendar is often visualized as a wheel. Within this full circle, everything happens. But this circle is not the kind that keeps us going around and around on hollow repeat. Surely trauma on a deep-grooved loop, recurrent loss, is its own inner circle of hell, and this is not what God ever asks us to enter. Rather, this is the kind of circle that leads somewhere; not a senseless spiraling, but a deepening toward a bright center—deeper into the heart of God, whose love is ever steady toward us. As Benedictine sister Joan Chittister writes, "Every week of liturgical life brings us closer and closer to the heart of things, farther and farther away from the superficial."[3]

Sacred time invites us to mark the moments and seasons of our lives—no matter how difficult or dissonant—to say *this matters*. It invites us to participate in the expansive story of all things made new, and in this hope, to trust the cycling of the seasons, because if they can keep moving, so can we.

At its heart, sacred time sets a sure tempo against the spiraling chaos of our lives: Christ with us in life, Christ with us in death, and we with Christ in resurrection. This is the rhythm that remakes the world.

How do you stay steady in the middle of a story whose ending is unknown? How can any of us tolerate the tension of a risk-riddled world where any love is shadowed by the inevitability of loss? These were the questions that churned within me that day in the exam room. Maybe these are questions that churn within you. The question beneath the question: *These are the variables. Where is the constant?*

The constant is closer than we think. If the liturgical rhythms are our invitation to draw near to the heart of God, then the *I AM With Us* is the heartbeat, the enduring pulse and promise vibrating at the center of all things.

The promise has never been smooth nor safe passage. The divine promise is *presence*. Wherever we find ourselves in the drama of mortal time, the immortal God makes with us a covenant of constancy. The here and now—this moment, any moment—does not have to be a place in which we spiral alone. Rather, it can be a place of profound encounter as we receive the radical *with-ness* of God through any life, death, and resurrection of our own.

The vow of God is as absolute as it is near. It is as spiritual as it is somatic:

Inhale: *I AM*

Exhale: *With Us*

The variables of this life are many, yet this covenant of constancy is sure. The prompt, the practice, is to stay awake to it.

I had a long way to learn—and still do—in the practice of keeping sacred time. But in those moments of unknowing seemingly alone in the exam room, I knew this much: My courage was renewed as I considered God-with-us through it all. This promise of presence steadied me in the midst of a spiral, and this is a promise—perhaps the *only* promise—that holds for all of us. In whatever spiral we find ourselves, the *I AM* is *With Us* in anchoring, unbroken rhythm. Here is a heartbeat with no beginning and no end, whose love will not let us go and encircles all our days. Here, for all the turbulence of love against risk, for all the quaking uncertainties of a precarious world, we might find the steadiness we search for.

Here, we might find our life.

2

DARING TO EXPAND

Advent

I AM courage to love
With You in a world of risk

> When the self is surrendered—when we're not too tied to
> our own agenda, anger, fear, or desire to make things hap-
> pen our way—we are truly open to love. But be aware of the
> heart's propensity to clench and close.
>
> RICHARD ROHR, *The Divine Dance*

It would have been so much safer, of course, if God had just *not*.
If God had just said, *You know, we could, but why bother?* If God
had simply elected to keep the borders tight, to keep the Trinity
a closed circle for all eternity—exponential in being, brimming
over with self-sufficient enough.

But instead, God invoked the opening lines of every new
story: *Let us expand.* God sang it first, and the universe has never
stopped expanding since.

In these three words, we find the anthem of anyone who has
ever consented to the terrible risks of love. Expansion is an anthem that unleashes a story you can't unspeak. It unlocks a kingdom of contingencies, and you don't get a say over what such a
future holds.

Here it is, the paradox of all paradoxes, the cosmic catch: The more you love, the more is on the line. We spend much of our lives in the heart's calculus of taking chances—*should we, or shouldn't we?* What gift might be given? What might it cost us to have so much to lose? How do we decide if the love is worth the risk?

In pregnancy, the uterus does something no other muscle can do: it expands five hundred to a thousand times its original size to make room for new life. How much more so did God expand when he said, *Let us make room for the future of humankind*?

I imagine God in the beginning not just saying, *Let there be light*, but, *Let there be . . .* each one of us, speaking our names one by one into that primordial night. Every birth is an Advent, each one of us the dream of God.

That's a lot of love. That's a lot on the line.

And yet. "When stumped by a life choice," author Oliver Burkeman writes, "choose 'enlargement' over 'happiness.'"[1]

Will this make me happy? is too often our default metric. But perhaps a more telling question is: Will this choice meaningfully expand my life, my interior self?

Expansion is the great ask upon our innermost muscles: to stretch beyond the borders of the self toward others, making wide the way for deep connection, for contact with something that is other than ourselves. Whether the body stretches to make room for new life, or the heart to encompass greater connection and empathy, expansion is the active choice for growth. And as such, it is rarely comfortable.

It works and wearies deep muscle. It pushes us to the edge, imposing scars that mark such a stretch. It is the nature of expansion to create tension, to stretch, and so it is no wonder that we often resist it. And yet expansion is the way of growth.

It is also the way of Advent.

The God of Advent, so bent on being near those he loves, resolved to be born as the dependent of a Palestinian teenager living under occupation. A baby—burdened with every human vulnerability: nerve endings, a startle reflex, a newborn's stomach the size of an acorn and its accompanying bottomless hunger. The creator of the galaxies has to rediscover all he has made from scratch, starting with the basic realization that those ten wiggling toes actually belong to him. Surely this was not the easy, "happy" choice.

Genesis tells the story of God's radical choice for expansion over happiness, and the world is born. Advent echoes and reprises this divine choice, and the world is reborn. First, life from the womb of God, now, life from a woman who made a radical choice for expansion, not just over happiness, but over personal comfort, safety, and reputation. Expansion was the call, and against its many risks, the mother of God said yes—stretching her body as well as her imagination for just what kind of hope this might be, growing now within her.

Had she said no, she would not have faced public scrutiny or physical endangerment as an unmarried pregnant woman in her day would have faced. She would have been spared the empire's hunt for her blacklisted family, driving them to live the life of refugees on the run. And she would have never known the unthinkable loss of watching her firstborn take his last breath.

Her path would have been so much safer, perhaps easier and even happier, if Mary had just *not*. And yet she chose the growing edge, where our truest self and life will always be found. And this choice made way for the life of the world.

Within the liturgical year, there are celebratory seasons and preparatory seasons, and Advent is one of preparation. In these anticipatory weeks leading up to Christmas, Advent is a season of waiting, and growing in the waiting. It is also where the story of the sacred year begins. Perhaps because this is where all the best stories begin: with the dare to say yes to that which stretches us, and that which ultimately transforms.

Zach and I met in college and married not long after, which is to say we married young. I printed the wedding invitations myself and took a ruler and a silver Sharpie to the edges of every single one, a makeshift gilding. We danced to "Moon River"—"two drifters off to see the world," and we did, in our own way. We enjoyed life as the two of us enough that we had never tried to change it. It went this way for nearly a decade, and we packed a lot into that decade—dotting the country with moves for my work, his grad school, more work, more grad school.

While starting out life in upstate New York where he grew up, we learned to cook (and fight) together in our postage stamp apartment, smoothing out our newlywed differences and disputes like a rolling pin over risen dough. We bought a small fixer-upper on a government loan and spent our evenings and weekends ripping out orange shag carpet and sanding floors.

Our marriage went long distance for a few months while I moved to start a new editorial position at a magazine and Zach stayed to pack and sell the house. There, while in Orlando and waiting for him to join me, I thrifted a pair of wineglasses, green like sea glass, but then I broke one and I hated to see the other like that—uncoupled in the cabinet—so I broke that one, too. Smashed it on the back stone patio like an iconoclast, swept it into the trash, and felt better. He and the dog arrived with the moving truck a few weeks later.

While in Michigan, we became mug club members at our neighborhood brewery, and our bartenders started calling us "the hackers," since we were always typing away on manuscripts and research papers. We spent many years like this—the two of us, typing side by side toward our respective ambitions. I won't glamorize this. It is never simple for two people sharing a life to discern just what shape that life will take—where they will live, which geo-time-financial-specific opportunity will be supported and which will have to wait, who will take the dog out and keep a running list of what's in the fridge at all times, the emotional-logistical choreography that must be managed to compose a mutual life.

Still, we were comfortable in the life we had built together. Ten years into married life, we had no imagination for anything beyond a table for two.

I remember once meeting Zach for dinner at one of our favorite local spots in Michigan, arriving separately. We were each coming straight from full-day events of our respective work. I was presenting new titles at a publishing sales conference, and Zach was presenting a paper at an academic conference, both in town. We'd shared happy-hour wine and mushroom pizza at this restaurant plenty of times, but I remember this one distinctly, because it felt significant and sexy to meet this beautiful person at dinner, he in his blue suit and me in my black midi dress, and to depart separately even though we'd be brushing our teeth elbow to elbow at home in a matter of minutes. It also felt iconic of the life we'd made together. We were two solitudes greeting, as Rainer Maria Rilke says—each our own, but so much better together. The space between us, the steady base of support from which we drew courage to venture out into our personal ambitions, emboldening us to take risks where we might otherwise not.

Then we moved south for the duration of Zach's doctoral program at the University of Tennessee, and he would soon be defending his dissertation and venturing into the academic job market. I was working through a seminary degree and had been promoted to a leadership position in my publishing program, and split my time between my home office, driving to Nashville for business, and flying back to our headquarter offices in the Midwest.

We had been in this together a long time: becoming one. But never before had we tried this: becoming three. It would take practice. A lifetime of practice, for this particular extravagance of expansion.

This will always be the ask of Advent: Do you dare to reach beyond the borders of the self for the communion that could be? Will you brave your yes to the unsettling transformation of expansion?

As for me, newly in my thirties, on the particular note of family planning, I was still stumped.

Perhaps it is the obvious, but let me state it just the same: There are many ways for a life to expand. Some will do so through this particular muscle of women, though pregnancy is far from the exclusive icon of expansion, neither is it the primary metaphor. The stretching of a belly is no sure equivalence to the stretching of the heart, and the heart that stretches may never manifest itself in the body.

Yet for all of us, this much is true: "Our hearts are muscles made to stretch," Laura Kelly Fanucci writes.[2]

I like this image, its reversal of sentimentalism, revealing the heart not as some soft abstraction but as a structured strength—a ribbed, chambered thing. The very muscle of expansion.

We stretch by reaching toward each other—by reaching out from the solo act into the plural "we," the pronoun God loves most. Life is long, the feast is wide, and we are meant for keeping it together. Our hearts are a muscle made in the image of God,

made for connection. And there are so many ways of being kindred.

We enact our own advents every time we brave reaching beyond the borders of the self toward each other. Expansion is the
anthem of anyone who is "brave enough to break your own
heart."[3] Every time we reach toward each other—considering
the risk, compelled by love—we sing its anthem anew.

Of course, there are just as many ways to expand as there are
ways to resist such a stretching of the borders of the self. And I
was feeling this resistance.

I come from a full house. I grew up as the middle of three
sisters, and after we all left the house for college, my parents became foster parents, which is how my two younger brothers became part of our family. Yet as a kid, I don't have any memory of
playing "mom" to my stuffed animals or little sister. As a college
student, I had all sorts of fantasies about what the future would
hold, but children were the silent omission in these visions. Now,
a decade into our life together, the desire had still not kicked in,
as I vaguely supposed it might. The starting status for both Zach
and me had not evolved from where it had begun: You want kids?
Sure, we felt, *someday*.

The question of discernment in this particular realm was real
to us and we wrestled with it, even if it carried the residue of fear
from our faith upbringings that we might somehow "miss" the
will of God and get it "wrong."

The magnetic pull toward pregnancy and parenting that I per-
ceived in others held no charge for me, was even perhaps charged
in the other direction. As an introverted individualist, I had only
had the experience of belonging to myself, and I distinctly dis-
liked the demands having a baby would make on my body, my

time, my sense of self, not to mention I was terrified of labor. We thought about adoption, but that, too, raised its own set of complexities.

Then there was the question of ethics—bring a baby into what kind of world, again?

And then there was a deeper current working my fear. I believed the mythology that the movement from woman to mother was the movement of a downgrade, a lessening of self. And I did not want to be reduced, as I felt then, to the trappings of banality that felt so inherent to motherhood—sticky high chairs and bottle schedules, dark under-eyes and dry shampoo. I wanted to *ascend,* to be left alone to my personal ambition and autonomy.

After all, ascension is more comfortable than expansion. It asks far less of us. Yet ascension is only a statement on height, not to be confused nor conflated with growth.

I would go home from baby showers relieved and self-congratulatory that I couldn't identify any of the breastfeeding or diaper-changing contraptions that the other moms all lauded as lifesaving. I was relieved that such meticulosity had no hold on me, that I could make my safe exit back to my Outlook calendar color codes and TSA PreCheck life, as if this was inherently more exhilarating.

It is ugly to admit this, but it is true. I wanted to write it all off as basic. But even this was code. "Basic" was really just a euphemistic catchall for what I really believed: This was *beneath* me.

Now I know there is a name for what spooked me so, that spooks many an individualist: the high-proof dependency of a life that so comprehensively, nonnegotiably relies on yours. To my cherished individualism, such sheer dependency was a stigma, a liability, an embarrassment, but more than anything, it triggered a raw-nerve kind of fear.

I was afraid of stretching and everything it would ask of me, take from me. I was afraid that parenthood would make less of me. I was afraid motherhood for me would be not an expansion but an override of the self—of my autonomy and freedoms, capacity for personal thought, the inner castle in which I felt most at home. I was afraid of falling into this predictable plotline of a woman's becoming, afraid it meant giving up my own plot.

Stretching always asks much of us, and it's no wonder we resist it when we do. But what if we dared to imagine the gift on the other side?

For a long time, we were preoccupied with the life that we already had, until my grandmother got sick and time went still. I was in the airport coming home from work in California when I got the call, and I cried the fast, hot tears of oblivion as if I were in the privacy and safety of my bedroom and not a crowded terminal in Atlanta. I rerouted my flight to go be with her in Baltimore as she entered hospice.

She was the matriarch of our family—my mother kept her maiden name and gave it to me, and I had also kept it as part of my name after we married—and the first grandparent I lost as an adult. For the first time, I had to reckon with a world without her, and for the first time, I felt the hard-stop edges of my nebulous "someday" plans for children she would now never get to meet.

My mother's mother was a lifelong Lutheran, a self-described "pushy old broad" who often took charge and just as often got in trouble for it, who staged interventions and steered synod committees and made no apology for what she wanted. Peg Sheeler once turned down a date with the dark-haired boy who rode up on his motorcycle to ask her out. "I don't want to go out with you," she said. "I want to go out with the other one—your red-headed friend." It's impossible to remember her without hearing her laugh—loud and long—which she did often, because she married that redhead and he could get her going like no one else.

In an era where most married women stayed home, she was a nurse and later a program director who testified before congressional committees for better public health funding for the aging. She advocated for her family and friends through her favorite spiritual practice of "benevolent meddling,"[4] and for herself, when upon retirement age she was told she did not qualify for a pension because she was a woman (she got her pension).

She believed in silver serving ware (paper plates were anathema), letting the little things roll off, and keeping confidences—whether you were one of her grands or Zelda Fitzgerald herself, who was in her care at the psych ward at the end of her days, though I never heard any stories. All of us remember her saying, "What difference does it make?" and, "No lives were lost." And she knew what it meant to lose.

She married the love of her life and then braved half a lifetime without him, made a widow too young—only in her fifties—by a stroke. She was a woman on intimate terms with loss, but she never stopped living. She fixed her hair every morning, invited herself over for dinner, and hosted epic dinner parties herself—setting the table so long she'd have to walk out the side door and in another just to pass the scalloped potatoes. She never stopped laughing loudly, and she would take you to task if you ever tried to steal the lunch bill. She traveled some, and small talk with strangers along the way would turn into pen pals for life. My mother used to come over and count her Christmas cards every year—topping one hundred, year after year. She was everyone's Aunt Peg, even though she had no siblings of her own.

I will long remember Reverend Anne, her pastor, at her deathbed in her tartan skirt and clerical collar, saying, "A lot of people fold in on themselves—they curve inward—as they age. Peg wasn't one of them. She never stopped reaching out."

Such is the sacred work of expansion.

Reverend Anne was right. Some might say Peg lived a small, ordinary life, but her radius of kin never stopped its outward movement. The outer rim of her capacity for human connection never calcified like it does for some people, like it so often did for me.

Perhaps that's the trick. Gravity will get us in the end. No matter how a life rises, no matter how long its days or how high its ascension, our future is inevitably down—a return to dust, a descent to its vertical end. We are all citizens of a universe suspended in free fall, as the oldest story is often told. What happened in Eden enacted a gravity that, without intervention, will end in a plummet every time.

This is a given.

Yet as long as there's breath in our lungs, even the inevitability of our vertical end can do nothing to stop us from outward expansion here and now. Nothing can keep us from the unfolding givenness of a life that blooms of love. Even when we're gone, this is the kind of love that carries on, rippling still through generations.

This is the gift.

I am drawn to the defiance of a life determined to reach out, out, out—afield of personal comforts and preferences, as far and wide as it can before it is brought low. It kindles something akin to aspiration in me. I like the brazenness of this, just as I love the "pushy" pluck of my grandmother and any inheritance that, I can only hope, has sifted down to me. Is there anything more death-defying than this: making the first move against the forces of gravity, pronouncing checkmate at the edge of the void?

I was starting to realize ascension is a solo act, an overhyped artifact of the hero's journey and its adulation of the linear. But a life that reaches out and out—hand stretching to another hand, first-person *I* stretching to plural *we*—is a journey of interconnection. A life gone radial: This is where the most enduring stories are told.

Out under the wind-swept blue of Big Sky Country, the soul cannot help but to expand. Maybe that's why I had hidden a pregnancy guidebook in my suitcase under a hoodie. Maybe I would get to it, maybe I wouldn't. Either way, I was standing at the shoreline, testing the waters.

It had been several years since my grandmother's death, each as full and demanding as the last. I was on a fly-fishing trip in Montana with a group of publishing industry colleagues, but our laptops were powered off that week. This was a week meant for retreat. We spent our days on the river, under the crisp October sun, and our nights huddled around the bonfire crackling under the Big Sky. We ate bison burgers and scouted for hawks on the porch with our coffee and gripped each other's shoulders as we stepped into ridiculously oversized waders.

I liked Tina at first meeting. I knew her so far only as an executive at another publisher—tall, bright-eyed, and at ease in her authority in a way that few people with executive power often are. She was the only woman among us who brought her own waders. I learned she is part of a women's fly-fishing group. I knew it was her signature on many a book deal that had beat me out. But I did not know that her husband's funeral was not a week past, which she shared with the group at dinner introductions our first night.

Deeper into the week, after we'd river-bonded and breakfasted with our morning bed head, I found myself sitting next to Tina at the fire. She was kind and direct, asked me about Zach, and then about family plans, which startled me at first, but then as my friend Mandy says, the firepit has a way of turning into an al fresco confessional.[5] So I told her we wanted to get through the logistics of Zach's doctoral program and a job-search-dependent move first.

"Babies are easy to move," she said. "It's when they're older that it gets tough to move kids around. But when they're little, you'll be just fine." She told me she raised her kids with the help of a live-in nanny, how there was no way she could've done it on her own. She viewed their nanny's help and love as a "double gift" to their sons. They were in their thirties, both had careers they weren't giving up, and they knew they wanted a family, so they simply had to get started. She told me all of this with open-faced objectivity. They simply made it work.

The fire warmed us both, and I realized it was a circle. She was not actually speaking to me, but to a young, tall, bright-eyed woman with big choices ahead of her. She was calling back over her shoulder to her younger self, speaking surefire confidence to the choices she made that led to the loves of her life, even now. It was happenstance that I was here; I was just a passerby, catching her words on the wind.

But in her certainty, I dared not miss the signal: For whatever the future holds, we all have in our power the ability to make something beautiful, to defy death by refusing to leave our life unlived. This from a woman whose husband's funeral was not a week past. This from the kind of person one should always listen to: a woman with no regrets.

"However terrible our sorrow may be," Kathryn Schulz writes in *Lost and Found*, "we understand that it is made in the image of love."[6]

Back at the airport saying our goodbyes in the terminal, we were all out of our waders and back in our weekday clothes. Tina had transformed from a fly-fisher woman in flannel and ball cap to a publishing executive in her tall black wardrobe. Someone commented on her necklace—a collection of silver charms, some miniature silver trout among them. I noticed a slim pendant-like urn at the center of the strand, near her heart. She patted it gently and said, "I'm keeping him with me. Just for a while."

The next weekend, I spent all Saturday on the couch, reading the book I had brought but had not read in Montana.

A few weeks later, at a Halloween party, a two-year-old mistook me for Mom, hugging my legs with full toddler might, until his realization sparked tiny horror and laughter in the adults. It was a fleeting moment, a party anecdote, but it reminded me of something, and its sensation held a certain staying power.

When I was little, my dad—who was an Eagle Scout, who knows trees by their Latin names and presses their leaves inside old books—used to dot our index fingers with sugar water to entice the summer's tiger swallowtail butterflies to land. It felt like that: the thrill of being chosen by a wild thing.

It was one stop short of desire—not full-fledged want, but wonder. Like that of a gap-toothed kid standing in a meadow, the open air of expectation on her palm, waiting for wings.

A friend once described becoming a mother to me like this: "I discovered whole new rooms in the house." I liked that image, a certain expansiveness, rather than the closed-in constriction I was afraid of.

I liked the idea that I might have dimensions yet unknown within myself to discover, to be awakened. And I liked the idea that, after a decade together, Zach, too, might have dimensions unknown that I had yet to meet. Here was a new spark: something to look forward to.

Where there was once the sharp tang of resistance, in the way that any of us fear what is unknown, there was now openness. What if a great becoming was yet ahead of me?

We calculated with pure pragmatics. We didn't want to have a newborn in the house before Zach had finished his doctorate, and we knew we'd be moving once he got out into the job market, so we arrived on a rough timeline of *not before x.* But having never tried before, we had no way of knowing how long it would take, or even if we could. So it wasn't a decision to *try,* yet still a major decision for us not to *prevent.* No pressure and no expectation, or so we thought.

We weren't starting a family—we already were one—but perhaps we were expanding what our family might be. Desire is not meant to be summoned on demand, so there was none for me yet, only a decision: *Let's draw the circle wider.*

The first pregnancy test came back negative, but I didn't believe it. The test had not expired, but it had been in our cabinet for a while. The familiar symptoms of my cycle were present, but my body was telling me this was something other, something new. I was so tired.

When I finally got my courage up to buy more tests at the pharmacy, I knew before I even looked.

How can such a predictable plotline feel so astonishing?

Suddenly I was a woman on the bathroom floor, knees on white tile, kneeling before the bigness of it all. I wept not because it was bad news, but because it was so big—bigger than I was prepared to take in on a workday morning. It was beautiful, this sudden knowing that my body was participating in an enduring mystery. It was also sooner than I ever expected. There was so much I wanted to do, so many things we had hoped to get in order before we got here.

"What are you feeling?" I asked Zach later, after the revelation, after we shared together in the full-spectrum astonishment of shock, joy, wonder.

"The chaos of joy," he said, blue eyes sparkling as if it were a dare. And perhaps it was.

Here is God—hovering over the waters, saying the gutsy part out loud into a cosmos of contingencies: "Let us risk. Let us chance the chaos of our joy." And look where that got us— a world riddled with beauty, ruin, and redemption, all of it. Green comets, grand sequoias, sisters who shave their heads in radiation solidarity, headlines that'll make you weep in the middle of a workday.

Not even God gets to pick and choose. A dare indeed.

Here are you and I and every one of us—hovering over the primordial powers of human decision. *Should we, or shouldn't we?* We stand on this threshold for the joy of love, of human connection, yet we deliberate for the risk. I suppose there is chaos in all expansion, because there is chaos in risk. For all our hopes, we do not know how any story will go.

We chance the chaos of our joy every time we dare to reach out against the fear of rejection, vulnerability, or loss. We chance it all, every time we let ourselves get too attached, say "I love you" first, go scared, keep our heart open after it's been broken. Every decision to stay in the hard conversation with someone we love, ask that maybe-new-friend for their number, show up to that support group, stay for the awkward coffee hour, or ask for help is a gamble on the gift of human connection, against the risks of getting hurt.

"Sorry, life is just too busy right now."

"We need to talk."

"It's not looking good."

"This isn't working."

Should we, or shouldn't we? This is the constant calculus of the heart: The more we love, the more we stand to lose. Love against risk is the inaugural and enduring paradox—God faced it first, and now, so do we.

Madeleine L'Engle writes, "If I affirm that the universe was created by a power of love and that all creation is good, I am not proclaiming safety. Safety was never part of the promise. Creativity, yes; safety, no. All creativity is dangerous."[7]

Creating a life in which we are kindred will always require us to risk.

It was a morning appointment—clipboards and paper gowns, giddy nerves under fluorescent lights. The wand worked its magic over my belly, then inside, and suddenly we saw: a bright star within. Zach reached for my hand. But we had no warning for what would happen next. The heartbeat broke into the silence like water rushing, drawing the sharp inhale of surprise from both of us.

How can you not be astonished by the sound of a heartbeat within you that's not your own? This was no quiet annunciation; it was straight ambush. And wonder cannot help but to give wide way to joy.

It felt like meeting someone you've heard about for a long time, an encounter, after hearing only rumors. Sugar water on fingertips, the thrill of being chosen by a wild thing.

Such math is mad: Two become one, creating the third realm of a marriage. Two cells meet—an unseen event of incarnation—then we become triune. My cells, his, then new: In the space between us, made spacious by love, a beating heart had bloomed.

"I had been my whole life a bell," Annie Dillard writes, "and never knew it until I had been struck."[8]

A life holds many advents, many beginnings. Some of them have a sound.

My body grew gently as the first frost gathered. The second Sunday of Advent, the week of peace, we snuck into the balcony late for church, as usual, but I wanted to come.

Imagine four hundred years of silence, then an angel who says do not fear, an unmarried teenager who has every right and reason to fear, a spoken yes that will change the world, and a zygote who is our very beginning, beginning to grow in her womb. The one who inspired all breath, who spoke the word that set every atom shimmering, joining in verse—now consents to smallness.

So small, Advent is a story that at first only mitochondria can tell. So immense, so vast in consequence, here begins the reversal of entropy and the inauguration of all things new.

Who came up with this story? What kind of plot twist is this? Alpha and Omega as embryo. The infinity of all good things tucked into so tiny a cluster of cells, humming gently awake.

The God who imagines galaxies siphons such exponential being down, down, down into a molecule-small kingdom. Just to know what it's like to be born, just to be with us—even in this.

The Maker consents to being made, and he makes his sanctuary in the body of a woman.

If Genesis tells the story of the birth of time, then Advent tells the story of time being reborn, casting woman as genesis, her womb the place where the worlds were made.

What a wonder to think my body was reprising so sacred a story. My first trimester and Advent were braided together, and I was in awe of them both. This particular bend of the liturgical narrative was no longer outside observation for me; this was intimate participation, my body a theater of ultimate things.

I read every scrap about the first trimester and fetal development that I could, and everything kept referencing "the mother" until I finally realized, *That's me.* Never had I tried on this identity before. But here it was, unblushing, irrevocable.

Zach and I had been so overwhelmed by the gravity of decision that we now felt the grace of the decision being made for us. It felt easier to accept something outside of our timeline and control than to shoulder the burden of calculating the "right" choice at the "right" time. So for as conflicted as I had been before, I was now gliding on endorphins, cocreating with God—the only *me* I've ever known was suddenly a *we*—and awash in this astonishment. My body was now practicing a plurality it had never practiced in quite the same way before.

Where I had once been afraid of being constricted, my world made small, I now felt new worlds opening.

It would be so much easier, one could argue, if only we chose to play it safe. But playing it safe often ensures the story won't have a chance to begin. And Advent is nothing if not the story of beginnings, revealing a God who dares to expand, who chooses enlargement over happiness, no matter the chaos. This season shows us the astonishing view of a God gone radial, one who will never stop reaching toward his beloved, no matter the risks.

And so, in the true spirit of Advent, we find our courage to chance.

3

NAMING THE NIGHT

Advent and Christmas

*I AM the God who weeps
With You in the darkest night*

You cannot rush the night. But you can light candles.

DIANA BUTLER BASS

Life was a rumor, whispered in aching breasts and morning vertigo, wonder a daydream. My body, in some deep atrium, had become a shelter responsible for someone else's time, space, matter. Cells clustered and multiplied, spinal structure curved and formed, joy became an unexpected practice.

Joy, it should be said, is not my default setting. I'm the one who's sad that the good thing will soon be over even before the good thing has begun. Open my closet and you'll find every sleeve painted black. The longest playlist I've ever created, and love unironically, is titled "Melancholia." I have lived a life well acquainted with apprehension: that suspicious, reflexive bracing for the other shoe to drop.

Joy is not my default setting. Yet here I was, claiming it as mine.

I meted out my pregnancy-approved portion of coffee, as I did most mornings before work, the dog settling into a warm circle on my lap. Morning prayer is one of the basic liturgies in the Episcopal tradition, along with compline or evening prayer, and I had developed my own practice as a way of grounding me and sending me into my day so anchored.

I greeted God according to the name given to God by Hagar: "You are the God who sees me."

I echoed the call-and-response form of the liturgy in my own expression:

"Will you walk willing into the gift of this day?"

"I will, with God's help."

I voiced a prayer of release and a prayer of receiving—exhaling and letting go of all I could not control, inhaling and receiving all that I needed for today.

Later, I will wonder: Is it possible for prayer to become a trip wire in one's memory, a trigger of PTSD? If so, this was the one.

It was a Friday, a day to wrap up my work for the week, but then in the late afternoon I saw something I shouldn't: blood dotting the water, red as mercury in thermometer glass. Precaution told me I should call my ob-gyn, so I did, noting they'd soon be closing for the day. But the gentle voice on the other end of the line told me something more urgent, "You should go to the ER."

That seems extreme, I thought. Everything I read said a little spotting is normal and not to worry. And I believed it, with the pious optimism of someone who dares to believe the worst won't happen to them. I believed it so wholly that just days before, I had hardly blinked when I spotted slightly at our friends' house, at the baby shower for their twins, the one with the buffalo plaid and the sugared cranberries in cocktail glasses. I simply flushed the toilet and went back to the party, merry and bright.

Zach had just gotten home from campus and I told him, as the official spokesperson of the voice of reason, that everything was surely fine but we'd go in for peace of mind. He dropped me at the entrance so he could park and I walked through the glass double doors alone. It was only then that the thought asserted itself to me consciously, in a way that I couldn't swat away: *I wish my mom was here.*

In the exam room, everything was sharp: the right angles of so much white on white, harsh light, antiseptic air. But none as sharp as the silence when my legs were splayed, stirruped in chrome, and the technician whose name I don't know said nothing as her wand searched for an answer I braced to hear.

The tech darted her glance from the screen, which was tilted away from my view, and the darkness between my legs. I lay very still on paper that crinkled beneath my weight. Every part of me, clenched like a fist.

She removed the wand and snapped off her gloves.

"You can get dressed now," she said, impassive as a blinking cursor. "The doctor will be in shortly."

This is how it happened. I caught the echo before I heard the sound itself, because I saw it on the tech's face though I knew she had been meticulously trained to hide it: the sound of a life unspoken.

When I first heard the heartbeat at my ob-gyn's office, I saw a parachute of color spill forth, loosed to the world, gesturing wild-alive in the wind.

As I searched this woman's face for signs of life, I saw this footage lunge into reverse—all that color unspooled, cranked backward into brittle nothing.

And I knew: There would be no spool of things to come. Love that was supposed to have a long, storied future could only be experienced now in a single direction: looking over my shoulder.

There should have been sirens at a moment like this. Shouting paramedics, glass breaking, red lights reeling. But when the moment came, it was savage in its serenity.

The doctor returned and the kindness in his eyes was subtle as a bullhorn. This was prepandemic, though only just. We were still in the "before" times when microexpressions were still legible, when meaning could be deciphered like runes between laugh lines, lip reads, hard swallows.

"I'm so sorry," he said, though I knew his lines before he ever spoke them. "We couldn't find a heartbeat." It occurred to me then that, in his job, it was probably the third time this week he had said them.

It was the fourth week of Advent. The week of joy. Advent, the beginning, God-with-us. But no, for us, the end of a story that never had a true chance to begin. A story that was only beginning jackknifed, swerved back on itself. Time slammed violently shut.

It was worse than a declaration, though. The doctor did not actually give us definitive news. "It's still early," he said. "It's possible they just couldn't find the heartbeat—this happens sometimes. It's possible all is well. It's also possible that this was a missed miscarriage." A clinical term for what I came to realize is the body's greatest betrayal: when an event as ultimate as death occurs inside of you, and your body doesn't get the memo. When your hormones continue to multiply toward life, you continue in your fever dream of a future, unaware that the future has already been undone. How can it be that the organ responsible for new life can be on such indefensible speaking terms with the rest of your body? How can it be that life itself has left the building, and you never even knew?

His prescription was purgatory—wait a week, rest, and schedule a follow-up appointment with my OB.

There was nothing left to do but go home. Nothing to do but call our families and break the best and worst news all in the same sentence, even though crying took over any words I had as soon as my mom picked up the phone. My mother is a doer, a fixer, a fighter. It's her job, as a social worker, but it's deeper than that—in her DNA. It is her nature to ask for the manager and most of the time, the manager is God, and she is not afraid to take him to task. But death is The Great Unfair and for it, there is no fix. I hated that I had to break this news to her. I hated that I had to present her with the mortal problem that no amount of willpower or advocating could resolve.

Ours would have been the first grandchild on both sides. After nearly ten years together, and blessedly respectful parents who did not push or pry, we could not wait to tell them our happy news. Only now, that anticipated high transfigured, took on teeth, broke the skin of us all.

All over the world, the lectionary read from Luke. An angel appeared to Mary and said, "Do not be afraid, Mary. . . . You will . . . bear a son and you will name him Jesus. . . . He will reign over the house of Jacob forever, and of his kingdom there will be no end."

A beginning, a name, a kingdom.

But for us, an end before there was even a beginning. Annunciation inverted, joy returned to dust.

That night, a storm came, the freak collision of southern humidity and northern currents. So loud, the whip-crack of thunder, that the dog yelped with surprise, then charged down the long hallway howling at the door as if she could fight the sky. It was comical, and then lurchingly sad, to see her try. I loved her for it. Dark clouds cracked open, and water rushed heavy. Only in Tennessee—thunderstorms the week before Christmas. I feared we would lose power.

I lay in bed and tried not to think of the deepening divide that may or may not have been happening that very moment in my body: the only time we shared turning stale, distant, with every breath of mine, every missed heartbeat. Every exhale a fire bellow's blow, blowing so beloved a ship back from the shore of what could have been, returned to a stormy sea.

I remembered my peace during morning prayer—*Will you walk willing into the gift of this day? I will, with God's help.* I was either a fool, or I'd been tricked, tricked, tricked. And I was not a fool.

Now, on the other side of everything, I prayed again, with an edit. *I will walk willing,* I told God, into the come-what-may. *But I will not betray myself so much that I would name this day as a gift.* I would not profane the day by naming it what it is not.

In the beginning, that beautiful "before," Zach used to ask me, "Do you have any, like, *inklings?* Boy or girl? It seems like some people 'just know' these things." And I used to wave off the question, no, I'm no skeptic of the mystical, but no special word ever arrived for me.

Now, though, on the other side of loss, a knowledge swung in with certain heat.

Maybe it was women's intuition. Maybe it was the kind of clarity that is carried to shore by tides of grief. Maybe it was the impossibility of spending a lifetime with "it" the only available reference for one so fiercely loved, the impulse to personify and honor the human soul.

Or maybe it was something darker. Maybe I just wanted to spite the male-born-God whose birthday is the hinge of history, the God who won't give our daughter one.

That Sunday, we did not go to church. Instead, my husband the contrarian, the academic who should have been a lawyer, whose first word was no and always fights to have the last, held me in the morning light and told me he hates anything he cannot fight.

And he's right. What drains you of the last of your strength, as it turns out, is not the fight at all. It's the forfeit—the fightless surrender death demands. The realization that this is something you can only let happen to you.

We were desperate for ways to pass the time. We watched movies, our attention only half there. I tried to tie up loose ends at work—wrapping up manuscript edits, sorting through my inbox—before Christmas vacation. I did not take time off, because how would I have spent it? I didn't want to be left alone with my thoughts.

I stopped by the pharmacy and picked up some supplies as recommended from the internet (the hairpin turn of my compulsive search history, a story too sad for me to dwell on): heat wraps, maxi pads, a sort-of waterproof liner used for babies and bedwetting that I had trouble finding, so I asked the pixie-haired teenager at the front for help. "How old is the baby?" she said, scanning the shelves for sizing options.

I knew nothing about babies and their development. "Uh, just a regular baby." I flapped my arms vaguely as if that would convey what I was not able to put into words.

It was the longest week of our lives as we waited for the worst to happen, and the waiting was violence in slow motion.

At what moment, exactly, did her being cease its becoming? At what moment did the cells stop multiplying, slip into reverse? When did time turn back on itself, when did it start counting down instead of blooming forward?

Did it happen while we slept, just after midnight? Or in the morning while we waited for the coffee to steep? While I was shaving my armpits in the shower? While I was picking out the perfect reveal cards to give to our families on Christmas Day?

Front: "What do you give the parents who have everything?" Inside: "A promotion! Congratulations, Grandma and Grandpa!"

Grieving means even this, surrendering the details that would dignify, if only we could have known them. Time of death: something certain, something firm. But we could not know. All we knew, as we filled a hollow week with anxious time, is that here we were together yet quietly unstitching, the seam breaking between the quick and the dead.

This is powerlessness: knowing that so ultimate an event is happening inside of you, without your consent. This is sadness: knowing that there is nothing you can do to render death undone.

When Zach and I were dating, I used to call him my favorite stranger. It was a way for me to express the multitudes of this person I loved most, how I expected to spend a lifetime discovering and learning new layers of his being. Never did I assume I had him "pegged" or all figured out. He is my person and I know him better than anyone, yet he is a mystery that will never wholly belong to me. My favorite stranger.

But how do you mourn someone you never knew, someone who never really lived? How do you hold in two hands the dissonant truths that this person is part of you, yet will for a lifetime remain a stranger—a beloved whose life you will never behold?

Pregnancy loss is an invisible grief, yet it is a death in the family. There is no past to speak of, no eulogy to write, no stories you haven't heard before to be told at the wake. Rather, it is the death of the future. Death of the story of us that could have been, should have been.

"Death was not ever meant to come before the day of birth, never," writes author and psychotherapist Christy Angelle Bauman.[1] And yet it does, commonly. It is well known that one in four pregnancies ends in miscarriage, yet the grief of such an intimate loss is wildly underrecognized.

In pregnancy loss, you experience death in your body in a most intimate way, and yet you keep living, and this can be a singular pain. Your body becomes the place where life was wanted, but then the place where death has happened. What was once God-breathed is now body-emptied. And yet, someone still has to defrost the chicken, talk about the weather with your pharmacist, go to meetings that should have been emails and happy hours and other people's baby showers pretending that the ultimate has not just happened, when of course it has. The loss itself is the first grief, and then the burden of pretense becomes the second. As any good therapist will tell you, there is a clinical name for the experience of our pain going unseen, and it is trauma.

Friday finally arrived, and I put on my comfiest sweater and Zach drove me to the clinic for our follow-up appointment. They sent in a social worker first with a clipboard of personal questions that she asked me with aggressive eye contact, pen poised.

"Do you have any thoughts of harming yourself or anyone else?"

"No," I said.

"Are you having any trouble sleeping? Any recurring dreams of The Miscarriage?" I heard her words as a proper subject noun, but this was someone else's vocabulary, not mine. Even after a week of trying on this tragedy, of anticipating the worst, I was genuinely surprised.

"Well, no, that's what we're here to find out." And then I understood. There would be no heartbeat today, either. I was the only one who did not realize this.

Blue paper gown again, bare legs prickling, I tried to focus on the warmth of my sweater as the wand searched inside of me again. I tried to forget the way I used to pray.

This doctor didn't shield the screen from me like they did at the ER. On the screen I saw her like a star that has died, returned to the final night. She was still there, but she was a light faded, sleeping in the galaxy of her quiet own.

When I was dressed again, when the word had been spoken and so made real, the doctor said to me, "I'm going to ask you a difficult question." I nodded. "Would you like to have a picture?"

No, I shook my head, no. I didn't need one to remember.

The doctor said I had options, as if the sovereignty of choice were a power that still belonged to me. He said I could go in for surgical removal, take a pill to hurry nature along, or try something called "expectant management," which is what he recommended, and ultimately what I chose. This word "choice" seemed to suggest I was still expecting, which I was, though we were on the B-side now. It also appeared to suggest that death is something that can be mortally managed, like a retirement fund or an expense report, and that was a consolation I could neither accept nor believe.

The glass doors opened and we stepped out of the clinic's artificial light into the southern winter sun, where the sky was an unforgivable blue.

While much of the world waited for God to be born, I was sent home to deliver death. So then came more waiting. And then came the losing. For me it was the Saturday before Christmas, Advent's week of joy, on winter solstice, the darkest, longest night of the year.

Unto us a child is born.

Unto us a child is taken.

Just beyond the industrial tracks and under the overpasses from where we lived, Knoxville's downtown square was decked with Christmas lights. Our neighborhood brewery had transformed into a courtyard Christkindlmarkt, with its illuminated trees and firepits blazing. Evergreens adorned the altar at our church. We didn't have a tree, as we always traveled to see family for Christmas, but I had unwrapped our crèche collection weeks ago. The holy family seemed to watch my every move in our tiny apartment. Now I just wanted to smash them.

Advent comes from the Latin word *adventus,* meaning "coming, arrival." It is traditionally known as the season of light, a gathering glow that is promised to overcome in this drama of light and darkness. It is a season of preparation: four Sundays of lighting another candle on the Advent wreath, culminating in the birth of God—the light of the world crowning like the sun herself over the sea.

But this was no arrival. We were awaiting departure, a place where light was no consolation, it was only crass. I could handle the honest dark. What I couldn't handle was dishonest pretense.

And it seemed everything around me was steeped in ritual devoted to cheer: dressing the tree, lighting the candles, baking the sugar cookies. But the rituals I needed most were the ones I didn't have: something to help me give honest observance of so intimately painful and private a loss.

Then I found one in an unexpected place.

It was the Saturday before Christmas, on the eve of the pandemic in the US, though we didn't know it yet. It had been nearly a week since we lost the heartbeat, and I was still waiting for my body to do what it needed to do. I remember sitting upright on the couch where I'd been living for the week when I read that today was the winter solstice.

Tonight, the earth's North Pole would reach its uttermost tilt away from the sun, ushering the northern hemisphere into the darkest night of the year. The winter solstice, I read, marks both the longest night as well as the beginning of its slow-laboring rebirth as the light gathers force until summer solstice, the longest day of the year. But first, for three days, the sun would appear to stand still. Together, the solstices serve as hinge-points of the year, equidistant symbols of death and rebirth, and are celebrated the world over.

I was vaguely familiar with the solstices previously, but suddenly I was reading with a hunger and I couldn't stop. In a distant time past, I read on one website, the sun entered its winter solstice while passing in front of Capricorn, the oldest known constellation. Capricorn was believed to be the gate of the gods, the threshold where newly departed souls made their passage into the beyond.

Suddenly I wondered if she would make her passage tonight.

I remembered some friends telling me about their winter solstice ceremony they host every year. They set a long table, and after a meal, guests are invited to write on slips of paper anything that has darkened their year, anything they would like to let go of, be free of, as they enter the new year. Fears, secrets, sins, burdens or beliefs that have hung heavy. They pass around a basket of fresh herbs and greenery—rosemary and sage, lavender and pine, each traditionally representing a particular theme: gratitude, forgiveness, peace. Each participant chooses a sprig to go with their scrap of paper, then tucks it gently into a square of burlap, tied with twine. And then they circle the bonfire together, surrendering the darkness they have so named to the flames. They call it a releasing ceremony.

That's exactly what I wanted. Ritual. Release. Something to burn. I didn't want to euphemize my grief, and I could not continue to celebrate the season of light where there was none for me. And if I could not control the darkness, I could at least name the night. I could witness it for what it was, and so give my grief the kindness of borders, naming becoming a frame for what would otherwise be only wilding shadow.

"I want to do this," I told Zach about the winter solstice rituals I was reading about.

"Let's do it tonight," he said. "I'll light a fire."

In the Victorian era, death happened at home, without the mediation of modern medicine, and families stopped the clocks at the hour of death. In Latin, "solstice" means "sun set still." Ours was an invisible death, an invisible grief, but the sun would stop her time for us. And I felt this empathy for what it was: cosmic. Even if only for tonight.

Our church, our city's downtown streets, everywhere I went seemed to be decked in so much light and I did not want to see it. Looking the longest night bold in the eye felt more truthful to me. The sun stilled her ascent, and her darkness was honest. As poet Jane Kenyon writes, "If it's darkness we're having, let it be extravagant."[2]

And so it was Saturday night, opening weekend for the new *Star Wars*, and I was eating a burrito bowl at a crowded strip mall twenty minutes before showtime. Life had introduced itself softly, now death did the same. It began with a quiet brushfire in my belly, where a beating heart should be.

The theater was packed, and our seats were in the middle. I was relieved to have some other story to step into for a while, to be preoccupied with someone else's stakes.

Somewhere in the middle of the film, Rey was fighting assailants on treacherous water on an ocean moon. The waves were a living thing, slow-moving slabs of gray and tornado green, making Rey so very small. Making me feel queasy myself. That's when the brushfire turned into something low and serrated, something sharper, and I excused myself, slipping past a dozen knees on my way out.

The restroom was empty, and I was relieved. There was no one there but me—*us*? I didn't know what words to use anymore.

I shut the stall and my body clenched again, some screw tightening deep within, bending me over. I don't know how long I was there for. All I know is that when I gathered myself again and got up, I knew what I would see when I looked, and I did. The future was bright, now it was too bright to bear, and it was leaving, leaving me. Two pink lines were never meant to give way to this: the color of life, redacted.

There was something else, too. Instinctively, I made the sign of the cross. We had only this moment. There were no last words, no eulogy, no funeral singers. Only an automatic flush and its sonic echoes in an empty cinema bathroom in east Tennessee.

My senses scrambled for reference points, cohesion. I was tossed like Rey among the elements: wind and waves, moon tides, blood and water. I was priestess of the requiem, a baptism, a water burial. A midwife, an undertaker, guiding passage of birth and death. I was a survivor with a tote bag full of drugstore supplies and the time had come to use them: heat wraps, extra-strength Advil, maxi pads. I was a woman washing her hands at the end of the world, while Whitney Houston launched into a key change from plastic speakers over chipped public restroom mirrors.

Popcorn butter salted the air. My eyes had to readjust to the dark theater where I jockeyed past the knees of strangers who would never know what ultimate things had just transpired. For me, apocalypse. The sudden presence of an absence. For them, Saturday night nostalgia in a galaxy far, far away.

"Are you okay?" Zach whispered as I settled into my seat.

"Yeah," I said, squeezing his hand. I did not tell him, not then. I hadn't even told myself; some protective impulse of magical thinking had sprung into action and taken over. The realization of what I had just seen came as a missed connection. It did not register in the moment, only studded itself in my subconscious as a question—*could it be?*—but it reverse-faded into clarity as the evening went on.

When she entered this life, it was through our togetherness. But when she left, I was her witness alone. Maybe that's why I wanted to cross her.

Meanwhile, outside the dark of the theater, the sun had begun its decided descent.

I told Zach after the movie, on our way home. My body felt wondrously better than even an hour before, having done what it needed to do, which seems strange to say but it was true, so I said it. He just wanted to make sure I was okay.

"I'll light the fire," he said, and even in the dark I could see his temples pulse and pulse.

If you would have driven by our house that night, turning left from the highway under the tangled overpasses, right over the railroad tracks, you might have seen a curious scene: two people holding each other as if in a trust fall before a blazing grill fire. The sky above them a clean, cloudless sweep of stars.

We walked to the neighborhood community garden and snapped rosemary sprigs in the dark. I got a beer because there was no longer any reason not to. We went makeshift and made a ritual of our own.

In the winter cold, we named the death of our hope, and fed it to the fire. We held hands and dropped in fistfuls of fresh rosemary. We took turns taking bitter index of the ways this year had left us wounded, emptied, and let the smoke gather in our hair. We watched the sparks, and in their warmth found haven in the honest dark.

"The stars are not wanted now; put out every one," the final stanza of W. H. Auden's "Funeral Blues" reads. "Pack up the moon and dismantle the sun."[3]

Tomorrow was Sunday, commencing Advent's week of peace, the lighting of the final candle, bringing us into Christmas week. That night, the fire was our way of saying so many things we didn't yet have the words for. One of them: *We'll make our own peace, thank you very much. And we'll make it by burning and walking away.*

There was no thrill of hope here. Only a fire to tend, and a long way until dawn.

For the first time in my life, I did not go to the Christmas Eve service. I couldn't stomach that kind of joy. I couldn't fathom singing "Silent Night" as we did every year, everyone passing the light candle to candle, person to person, until the sanctuary was aglow and the crescendo cresting, "Sleep in heavenly peace." I couldn't participate straight-faced in this remembrance of the ultimate pregnancy narrative, this birth story to end all birth stories, in which God made it from embryo to first howling breath—but my daughter did not.

Cole Arthur Riley writes, "There is no greater exhaustion than a charade of spirituality."[4] I simply had no energy to keep up the charade.

In a season of all things merry and bright, the winter solstice gave me the gift of witness. The longest night gave me permission to hold space for darkness and death when I needed it most. At their best, this is what rituals of grief do for all of us. Amanda Held Opelt writes, "My experience is that rituals introduce a healthy rhythm of exposure to the grief. They allow us to let off emotional steam at specific moments. With a ritual, you willingly confront your losses head-on a few times a day or a few times a week, so that you don't have to be beholden to them all the time. Rituals name and order the chaos of our emotions."[5]

So much of Western society is designed to deny the night. We are not well versed in the shadows that define the human experience alongside the light. When it comes to anything that cries of our mortality, our language is embarrassingly impoverished. Rather, we are told in so very many ways: *Your pain does not belong here.* Keep it private, we are told, far away from polite company. Stuff it down and suck it up. And get over it as quickly as possible. This is the essence of toxic positivity: the pressure to keep up the charade that all is well when nothing is okay.

But this cheap counsel speaks against the grain of the universe, and none of us mortals are a match for that. "Every twenty-four hours," Anglican priest Tish Harrison Warren writes, "nighttime gives us a chance to practice embracing our own vulnerability."[6]

The hours, the tides, the seasons and solstices all testify to the elemental truth that life, death, and liminality all belong in our shared circle of time. Even the story of the Incarnation, against which I was now bracing, was not exempt from the longest night. It might be heavenly peace for now, skin-to-skin on a silent night, but I knew this same God-child would one day be marred unrecognizable, that his mother would watch powerless as God's own heart stopped beating. This, too, was part of the story.

Novelist D. H. Lawrence writes, "We *must* get back into . . . vivid and nourishing relation to the cosmos. . . . We *must* once more practice the ritual of dawn and noon and sunset, the ritual of kindling fire and pouring water, the ritual of the first breath and the last."[7]

It is only human to seek consolation for our pain, but the consolations we crave most will never be found in making less of it. The greatest consolation will never be sourced in scrapping for bright sides, empty speculations of *why*, but in the full-stop validation: *Your pain is real. Your lament belongs.*

Look away, look away, says the artificial light of toxic positivity, *it's too much.*

No, the darkest night dared to counter, *this, too, is your life. Bear witness.*

When you're hurting, the only thing worse than the hurt itself is the intimate injury of being told your hurt isn't that bad, that your pain is somehow unjustified. There is no greater trauma than this invalidation when what you most need is empathetic witness. That's what Advent felt like to me.

But it wasn't Advent itself I was bucking against. It was the saccharine, the spin, the half story with the full gloss that rendered this complex coming of God into one-dimensional joy that excludes all other experiences.

The Incarnation always brings good news, but it never minimizes the realness of our pain. Advent declares the hope that a light is coming, but first it declares the truth that the world right now is so very dark. In all the festivities of this season, the threads of Advent and Christmas are commonly confused. The celebration of Christmas only means so much if it bypasses the great waiting, the great groaning, of Advent itself. But this is where the story—and the sacred year itself—begins.

The first language of this expectant season is not bell carols but groaning—the audial ache of a hurting world.

The God of Advent is not a God of indifference, but the God who imagined mirror neurons into existence—the cell network responsible for so much of what makes us human, which is the basic ability to read and respond to the emotional needs of others. Every human encounter of empathy begins with mirror neurons firing in witness to pain.

It is fitting, then, that the sacred year begins with Advent. Human pain is the call—every nerve ending crying out. The Incarnation is the response—every mirror neuron of God firing, volcanic in awakening. God hears the crash and cries of our great fall and, like a mother, comes running. Emmanuel rushes through time and space to be not just near our hurt, but human with us in it.

What I had missed was the very essence of Advent: This is an entire season dedicated to hearing the hurt and naming the night. We are not just *allowed* to do so, we are openly called to do so. I just needed to discover this for myself.

4

REDEFINING RESILIENCE

Epiphany

I AM the heart of empathy
With You in both joy and pain

Only by learning to live in harmony with your contradic-
tions can you keep it all afloat.

AUDRE LORDE, *Sister Outsider*

If Advent is the anticipatory season of "Before" the birth of
Christ, then Epiphany commences the season of the "After."
The word stems from the Greek expression meaning "to reveal"
or "to come to light." And so the feast of Epiphany following
Christmas commences what is often called the season of light,
illuminating the gift of God for all people through a series of
revelations. First, a star that appeared to the Magi, then the baptism of Christ, the unfolding of his public miracles, and finally,
his transfiguration.

In my imagination, I see these revelations as stars—creating a
constellation in a dark world, just as the prophets had promised.

There's a curious story tucked into this season. When the
Christ child was forty days new, his parents brought him to the
temple to present him to God as was the Israelite custom for

the firstborn. They were met by a prophet who declared their son to be a light for all people, bringing salvation yet also division as this light would reveal the hearts of many. The text says Mary and Joseph were "amazed" at these words, but then the prophet turned and spoke to Mary, "and a sword will pierce your own soul too" (Luke 2:35).

Simeon spoke to her as a prophet, as one foretelling what was to come. Yet he also spoke to Mary as a mother, as one who held fierce hope for her son's well-being and protection in a hard world.

His words also speak to us, proclaiming the open contradiction of Epiphany:

The light has come! And a sword will pierce your heart also.
Salvation is here! And its revelation will not be easy.

Epiphany's light is a light that reveals all—the beautiful, the terrible, and the things we'd rather not think about at all. This is a light that levels just as Simeon leveled with Mary to say that the story of God is big enough for every conceivable both/and across the continuum of human experience.

This epiphany is intimate, as personal as it was to Mary, and admittedly sometimes unsettling—calling us to contend with the paradox of joy and pain.

Advent is the beginning of the sacred year, yet for us, Advent was where it had all ended. So as the calendar crossed into January, I felt this dissonance more than ever. I entered the New Year tenderly, as if walking into a hard wind. I stood defenseless on its threshold, and I did not kid myself by believing it would be a better, brighter era ahead, as if anyone is entitled to such things.

But I could commit to the only thing within my control: to practice my strength no matter what might come. I felt fierce about that much.

On New Year's Day, after a long brunch at my sister's, we went for a walk in the reservoir watershed. It's a family tradition, these walks. And it was good to get some fresh air, even if the sky was white and snowless. Brothers, sisters, and brothers-in-law piled into two cars and met at the trailhead, where we were intercepted by a breathless woman waving flyers.

"Excuse me," she said. "This gentleman just lost his dog this morning on the trail, and we're trying to help a neighbor out." The flyer showed a large, floppy-eared mixed breed of some kind, a cheek-to-cheek selfie with his grinning owner.

And suddenly my heart rate was rising, and her mission became mine. This was no longer a walk; this was a search party.

The forest was bare, a slight wind rustling the leaves in a sweep of sepia. We walked a path cut through thistle and bramble, quarry rock, staghorn sumac in its rust red. Everything brittle and stark and how I felt on the inside: hollowed out, fallow.

It was New Year's Day. A day for sleeping in and overstuffed omelets and the oxytocin of new beginnings. It was there in the woods that it occurred to me: This was postpartum. It was not a beginning, but it was definitely an *After.*

My sisters were up ahead, my brothers trailing behind, kicking roots and rocks as they went. I was in the middle, eyes scanning, in what was becoming a sort of fervent prayer. Senses on high alert because no one, human or creature, should be lost on day one of a new turn around the sun. We belong with the ones we love, and something in my grief was reaching out to the grief of this stranger in knowing his dog was lost in the woods all alone when he should have been safe and warm at home.

It was New Year's Day and we should have been basking, belly in gentle expansion, giddy with good news. My mother should have burst into happy tears upon hearing our news, gone to bed smiling. Instead, we were searching for a lost dog in a bare forest on a January morning. The future was now a ghost of Christmas past, haunting us all.

As engaged as I was in my silent search, it was my brother who spotted him first.

"Hey!" He whistled. "Here, boy!" We all turned and saw him: a panting, grinning dog ambling through brittle milkweed husks. There was a scurry and an uproar, and after much calling, clapping, and plying with granola bars, we were able to grab hold of the dog's collar. We held it fast all the way back to the car, where we called the number on the flyer, and I could hear the relief in the pitch of a voice on the other line.

New Year's Eve had been a hard one for me. Sitting cross-legged on the floor with my sisters and a charcuterie board, passing the hours with good wine and irreverent laughter while playing Bards Dispense Profanity, I wanted to forget, but I also didn't. Here it was: the final tick of the clock, crossing all of us over the threshold into not just a new year, but a new decade. And here it was, the tragedy of mortal time, in that she did not cross over with me. The midnight border marked a solid, unbreakable line now dividing me from her. You can't walk back from a line like that.

When midnight came, I knew with sadness that it was mine to move forward. It was hers to stay still, fixed in a moment that I could not access in the present anymore. Time was on the move and its tectonic plates were gently moving us apart. I was in the *After* now, alone in my body again.

We didn't get to bring our baby home. We would go home to an empty house.

But my heart felt the quiet lift of relief in knowing there was a homecoming today, even if it wasn't mine. Here was joy, here was sadness, cheek to cheek. It didn't need to be one or the other. I didn't have to deny the joy of another's union to validate the pain of not having the one I'd hoped for myself. What's more, I found I didn't want to.

Maybe love is like this, a search party to restore the belonging that has been lost. Flashlights and shouts in the forest, and most of all, hope for the finding and being found. Ram Dass writes, "We're all just walking each other home." Aren't we all a little lost in the woods, trying to get home? And isn't that what we all want for the ones we love?

When we find ourselves in difficult times, we each want to be the kind of person able to withstand them. We want to be people of resilience, tapping into that inner strength able to sustain us against destabilizing forces. Yet how we access and practice such a strength is the question.

"Time heals all wounds."

"One day you'll be 'over it.'"

"This, too, shall pass."

Some call it spiritual bypassing, overcomer culture, or toxic positivity, but by whatever name, we've all heard the scripts. And the language of bright-siding and brave-facing all presumes a linear mindset. The assumption that life is linear is a setup for all sorts of false promises: that personal progress is the reward for those who just push through, that we can make a clean getaway from past pain by simply hopping "over" it like a track hurdle. That the ideal life traces the pattern of the hero's journey—sure, you might face some setbacks, but from there, the only way forward is up. And maybe worst of all, this mindset ratifies the expectation that if your life is *not* a bright line rising steady to the right, you're doing it wrong.

Within this straight-line mindset so favored in the modern Western world, resilience is often presented as putting as much A-to-B distance between oneself and past pain as possible. But no one should have to hustle for their own healing.

A straight-line-to-the-top is too simplistic for the complex creatures that we are, and I cannot believe that our healing is so cleanly predictable that it can be charted on graph paper.

The cycle of the seasons, of both the earth and the sacred year, shows us there is no clean, straight line. There is only the slow-gathered accumulation of wisdom through the circle as we move through the seasons high and low, dignifying each through honest witness. If time is not linear but cyclical, authentic resilience is cultivated through braving the bend again and again, deepening with every new orbit. The strength we need most is sourced not in bouncing back or powering through or even fighting forward, but in holding in tension the highs and lows of the human experience by declaring, *This, too, is true.* True resilience will never be a project of denial, but rather one of open witness. We become more human when we choose not to make less of our pain.

This is precisely the way God became human: never to minimize our pain as overcomer hustlers are quick to prescribe, but rather to take on human skin and scars himself with us.

"Over it"—what an empty place to be, where nothing can touch you. I hope I'm never over the realness of loving another, even if this means enduring loss. I hope I'm never over the depths and empathy that love through loss has awakened in me. I hope I'm never over it because if you dim one set of colors in the color wheel of human experience, you will desaturate them all. And then you'd have to be over the bliss of first snows and blackberry cobbler and baby teeth. On the whole, I'd rather stay in it. I'd rather live in color—with the fullness of my humanity and the life cycle itself.

I'm starting to think this is the way of authentic resilience: not checking out of your life, or even powering through, but practicing the learned skill of staying in the tension, where deeper muscles are activated. It takes a certain kind of soul stamina to accept that joy and sorrow belong to each other just as the salt belongs to the sea. And so we find our resilience in holding these seemingly disparate realities and making our peace with the paradox by trusting it is all seen by God. We find our resilience in the soul-stretching acceptance of reality as it is, and the active resistance of toxic positivity as well as the defeatism of despair. Christians will recognize this as the virtue of hope, which equally resists the errors of presuming entitlement to future good and feeding the certainty that disaster is inevitable.

Despite what the overcomer narratives would have us believe, the onus is not solely on us for our record-time recovery. Rather, we can withstand any hardship so anchored by the sacred trust that God is *with* us through it all, every season, lush and low.

As it turns out, we are not fixed points on a graph. The human story is told not through orderly rows and columns, but through spirals and switchbacks.

We are circulating creatures living in a circulating universe. The world turns. The womb expands. The tides rise and fall, the moon waxes and wanes, the planets slow-dance the sky in their orbit, the body wakes and sleeps in circadian rhythm. The natural seasons and the liturgical seasons trace the same full circle movement again and again, carrying us in its current.

The very movements of our vital systems—blood coursing through vessels, breath flowing through our lungs—has a name that confesses as much: *circulation.* At a biological level, our lives are defined by its full circle movements. All living things follow in this precise narrative arc.

Yet there is a difference between going in circles, getting caught in a loop, and braving the bend again in such a way that deepens the wisdom and resilience of a life with each new orbit, each new layer.

I wanted to learn how to do the latter.

True healing relies on empathetic witness—for our trauma to be seen, heard, and validated—and that is the gift we received from friends and family in the wake of our loss.

When I called my sister Allison to break the news and cried on the phone, she cried with me. My friend Rachel sent me a giant white candle, with a note: "I hope your new year is a year of brightness." So we lit candles. I found a good therapist. We received the gift of listening ears, text check-ins, and homemade biscuits as only Tennesseans can make. Our loss opened up the kind of kindred conversations that happen when people have walked through similar pain.

When we told our priest what had happened, he met with us for coffee one morning over buttered sourdough and mugs that steamed in the morning chill. Father Aaron loves Tennessee Orange, Kentucky whiskey, and Celtic spirituality. When not in his vestment robes, he wears a wide-brim straw hat suitable for picking tomatoes at the urban farm his wife manages, or sneak-attack spraying his children with the garden hose. He's also been known to get a little fast and free with the holy water at baptisms, making a splash zone out of the first three pew rows at least.

But that morning he was serious.

"There's another part of the Christmas story," he said, "that often gets left out. The part no one wants to talk about."

And I knew what he was going to say before he said it. It's the part that never makes it into the Christmas pageant. The nativity scene that gets top billing is shadowed by an underbelly narrative of manhunt, massacre, refugee flight, exile.

A power-paranoid king hears rumors of a Messiah's birth and, fearing his throne will be threatened, commissions the execution of children. The Child King is born onto a blacklist. The holy family flees for their lives, becoming refugees in another country for untold years before the king finally dies and it is safe to return home.

The text says King Herod was "disturbed" (Matthew 2:3) to learn of this particular birth, "and all Jerusalem with him," because his ruthlessness was legend, and they knew they would pay the price of his fear. What follows is this deeply disturbing story about at-risk children that does not end the way we hope it will.

The way the Gospel of Matthew tells it, this unthinkable tragedy follows right on the heels of the Magi's visit.

Here was joy, here was sadness, that open contradiction again—cheek to cheek.

The immediate After of Epiphany is a story told through trauma. The light of the world has come, but no amount of sentimentalizing can paper over the aftershocks. While the star rises over the manger, the sky goes dark for the families of the innocents.

This narrative, traditionally known as the Massacre of Innocents, ends with a prophetic proclamation of lament:

A voice was heard in Ramah,
        wailing and loud lamentation,
Rachel weeping for her children;
        she refused to be consoled, because they are no more.
            (Matthew 2:18)

Rachel was the wife of Jacob, whose suffering is first recorded in Genesis as she died in childbirth. Jeremiah later refrains her lament as Israel, the children of God, are being led into Babylonian captivity. And now, generations later, her weeping echoes anew for the children who are taken by a jealous despot.

"I can't sit here and tell you that I know what to do with this," Father Aaron told us. "But we can't edit it out if we want the story to hold up, to have any integrity. I can tell you that every Christmas, knowing the families within our community as I do, I look out at the faces of our congregation and see the mothers who have lost."

Father Aaron is an avid admirer and collector of icons, and he choked up in what he said next. "When I look at the Theotokos," he said, speaking of the Mother and Child icons, "I see Rachel weeping still." Zach squeezed my hand under the table and now we were all trying to keep our composure, as our little table in the bakery had become a sacred place where we felt seen.

I was resentful of the Christmas narrative because I presumed its joy to be a mandate threatening to override the pain of my experience. I bristled against its warmth and glow because, in it, my grief felt invisible and invalidated. Mine was the particular pain of feeling unseen. But this was an assumption and oversimplification. If I looked closer, I found complexity. I found a story layered with the full-color spectrum of human experiences.

I thought of the prophet's words to Mary: "and a sword will pierce your own soul too." And I thought of the angel's greeting of "great joy" (Luke 2:10). Here was a story that held prophets rejoicing in the temple to meet the one they'd spent a lifetime waiting for. It also held the reckoning of a mother with the knowledge that her child would one day die. It held both Mary's Magnificat and Rachel's weeping.

Life is like this: a great shimmering color wheel of emotions that jostle against each other in surprising, sometimes unsettling ways. Time holds many memories, and anniversaries overlap and overlay the present. Life, death, and resurrection cycle through our days like the turning colors of a kaleidoscope. We weave in and out of bouts of brimming-over joy, impossible hope, and fragile fear.

Life is absurd—because so much happens and so little makes sense. And it is exquisite—because even as the kaleidoscope turns, look at all that color.

This is what Epiphany that year illuminated for me: In the aftershocks of suffering, the most important choice we can make is to accept the exquisite absurdity that pain and joy are both parts of a meaningful life.

Could I let joy be joy and sorrow be sorrow, however they each might be encountered in this sacred story as well as in my own? Could I follow the lead of the Spirit beyond the scripted binaries, into the wildlands where God's *withness* might meet us in both?

I wondered at the dissonance Mary must have endured in making sense of these proclamations. I wondered at whatever interior strength sustained her to hold both a sword and a star in her heart. While I had been bracing against Mary's joy, I now also saw her sorrow, illuminated by Epiphany's light. And the way this sacred story gave witness to the fullness of her experience began to make me feel seen in my own.

The rhythms of the sacred year turn like a kaleidoscope, the colors of each season transfiguring as time flows forward. It can be deeply painful when the liturgical moment grates against the emotions of our particular here and now. When the celebratory seasons seemingly hold joy for others but for us slammed doors, unsettling news, and control-shattering scares. When the seasons clash with our personal moment, it's easy to feel unseen and overlooked.

I think of my friend Emily—surrounded by family and candle-lit birthday cake—who cried out for them to stop midsong, because her birthday was anything but happy. Because she was supposed to be pregnant, but had delivered their baby girl early, knowing she would not live.

My friend Seth once led an Easter morning worship set—trumpeting key changes and all—hungover from the night before, just another night in the cycle of promising himself that tomorrow would be different.

Dale was young and healthy, despite some back pain, which he went to get checked out. Then his sister and my friend Natalie spent weeks fighting for hope after a lung infection turned septic and he was put on life support. The family said their goodbyes just before Christmas.

My mother-in-law miscarried on Good Friday and had her D and C scheduled for Holy Saturday. She is a pastor's wife, yet stayed home on Easter. As she told me, "While our church family celebrated the empty tomb, I was grieving my empty womb."

Life is nothing if not juxtaposition.

Yet even in this dissonance, the Incarnation bears a subversive hope, for it means God is always showing up in our real time. For the eternal God, all time—past, present, future—exists in the here and now.

For God, there is no moment that stands outside God's present. And so for us, there is no moment in which God's presence does not meet us. The prophets spoke of Jesus as a "man of sorrows" who was "acquainted with grief" (Isaiah 53:3), and so his sorrow greets our sorrow, just as his joy greets our joy. Divine empathy—the witness and *withness* of God—is always ready to meet us.

To all the overcomer narratives, to all the selective-memory "gospels" that tout resurrection but gloss over the death before it, I wanted to say, *If your version of reality can't hold my grief and rage and wilding, then there is no room for me in it.*

But a story that holds space for my grief as well as my joy, my pain as well as my peace, is a story that holds my attention. The expansive story is the story that holds my respect.

Even here, in the season that celebrates light, a voice goes up. An ancient mother sounds her lament. And for all the peace on earth, for all the sounding joys repeated, she will be heard.

We may never have a prophet tell us as much, but there are so many ways for a soul to be pierced. So many reasons to weep. And so many dark nights that convince us the light might come for others, but not for us. Yet like Rachel, whose cries echo through the centuries, and like Mary, whose heart held a sword as well as a song, our sorrow is sacred. And our witness is none other than God.

One morning in late January, a package arrived from my sisters. My sisters are especially into the arts of the analog. They make homemade brioche and buckwheat bread, play the piano and the ukulele, pen the most beautiful calligraphy cards I've ever seen.

Whatever they've sent me, I knew it would be a considered gift. Inside layers of bubble wrap and emerald green tissue paper, I found a small stained-glass triquetra—a Celtic symbol, a knot of three interlacing arches. This image has long been known as the Celtic-imagined shape of the Trinity: Father, Son, and Holy Spirit. Creator, Sustainer, Redeemer.

My sisters signed the simple card—in fine-point calligraphy— that came with it in a sort of trinitarian verse of its own: "Remembering with you, here for you, and hoping with you."

It is the sacred work of love to transcend the tenses, to break through all borders of past, present, and future.

I tacked it up at the window over the kitchen sink. The glass is blue and green, like earth and water, the first colors at the birth of time itself.

Every morning, I made my coffee in its view, and it became an accidental icon of sorts. Because whenever I looked at it, I could not help but look to the light beyond it, even during a time when I felt there was none for me. The triquetra shows me a God who is an unbroken circle. But in this divine communion, this interlacing of three, I started to notice something else, something new—God as a circle, yes, and within that circle, a space that is so very much like a womb.

In these quiet morning moments, I began to see a bright center—a space where God makes space for us. A space that represents our beginning and seals our belonging, an unseen sanctuary in which we live and move and have our being. Together they are Trinity, and together they sing and sway as Mother, hovering over the waters, womb expanding, at the beginning of time.

When the Scriptures speak of all things holding together in Christ, this womb-like space has become what I visualize. Because it visualizes what Love does for us, which is to take the risk of making room. Nothing that is lost does not come home here to rest—not lost dogs on New Year's Day, lost pregnancies during Advent, lost hope itself. Nothing that is broken does not find its wholeness here, in this bright orbital hem. No atom of creation is overlooked, left stranded. Rather, we are held, steadied and surrounded by a force of care.

I didn't have the words at the time to name this so directly, but I could intuit something here that came to me as consolation: God is a circle, the circle is a womb, and in her, all things hold together. And I certainly did not feel capable of holding things together on my own.

Maybe the liturgical year is just such a circle, just such a womb, capable of holding us together when we cannot do so on our own.

The particular shape of the Christian calendar casts time as a full circle—life, death, and resurrection. This is the Paschal mystery,[1] the undercurrent of everything. And it shows us that God is with us in our time. We are full-circle beings, created in the image of a full-circle God. In every moment, liturgical time extends the invitation to find points of contact and connection with the ancient story, one in which death is witnessed and loss honored, but never has the last word. Such sacred time invites us to practice resurrection, even while we bear the tragedies of mortal time.

We live in cycles of life, death, and rebirth until at last mortal time gives way to the completion of all things, which is Love declaring, "Behold! I am making all things new."

And that is why the cycle of the seasons can be trusted, because we know where they ultimately lead.

As Zach and I reckoned with the trauma of our loss, and experienced the gift of others bearing witness with us, I began to see the liturgical year as a radical expression of God's empathy toward us all. Surely this is the heart of the human effort behind envisioning the sacred year to begin with, as the church over the centuries foraged for ways to make sense of God-with-us in our time.

If human time is a story told by Love, then it must be big enough to hold everything. In a society hell-bent on keeping things upbeat and forward-looking positive, here was a story that said: *Your love, your loss, your liminality is all real, and it all belongs.* Here was a love that would never look away. A love that will never disdain, downplay, or make light of our pain. And conversely, will never invalidate or diminish our joy. A love that would only ever witness the full-spectrum color wheel of the human experience, with us in the greatest joys and deepest griefs and all shades in-between.

I was hurting profoundly. I was nowhere close to "over it." This would not be an overcomer story. But this much felt true: I could trust a love like that.

A mentor of mine once told me that authenticity is simply being loyal to yourself. So one weekend in midwinter, loyalty to myself and my needs meant making a last-minute trip to the mountains. Zach and I had been wanting to get away for months, but overloaded with work and studies, we had put it off. But now we needed it more than ever, so we packed the car and drove into the Smokies of Tennessee, arriving at a cabin with a porch view of a river.

Grief and health insurance and going back to work with everyone asking brightly, "How were your holidays?" was all so thorny and complicated. But here on the mountain, simplicity was the order of the day, and I could not have imagined how healing this would be. We packed a cooler with bacon and eggs and canned soup, and popped over to the little grocery store down the way for some chicken, Tennessee barbecue sauce, and fries from the frozen aisle. We grilled it all on the porch, and it was the best meal I'd had in a long time—perfectly unfussy pleasure on scalloped paper plates.

There was no Wi-Fi, so we tuned into quiet currents instead: river moss and rainwater, stacks of books and porch blankets, and a coffee pot on perpetual brew. We slept in, and in the morning, the cabin and its rafters were full-power golden. I sat under the eaves of the covered porch for hours, watching the hemlock branches tremor in the wind, Canada geese loudly performing their water landings on the sunlit river. Sometimes it's the quiet currents that tell the deepest truths. And in the quiet, I felt washed clean by the mountain air, the river rush, the woodsmoke and simplicity. I was remembering myself on the mountain. I was re-membering the woman who broke open not so long ago.

It was there on the covered porch that I reread Madeleine L'Engle's classic *A Wrinkle in Time*, following the impulse to return to old favorites. I have always felt a certain kinship with her writing, from childhood reads of the *Time* quintet to discovering in college *Walking on Water*, her incredible book on creativity.

A Wrinkle in Time follows teenage Meg, her little brother Charles Wallace, and friend Calvin in an interstellar search-and-rescue mission for their scientist father who has been captured by dark forces on another planet. The Library of America calls it "one of the most beloved and influential novels for young readers ever written."[2] Perhaps because Meg Murry is all of us—feeling awkward in her skin, glasses and braces, full of faults and angsty in her self-awareness of them, yet fiercely protective of those she loves. And in the end, it is this love that has the last word, a hope that is held out to all of us.

The novel, first published in 1962, was an odd bird among young adult fiction, as it did not shy away from what might be considered more "adult" topics. L'Engle deliberately declined to dumb the narrative down for young readers, instead trusting their imagination and intelligence to grasp big ideas in physics, philosophy, and religion. Most of all, she did not shield young minds from very real forces of darkness.

It would seem L'Engle, too, was suspect of linear thinking. "A straight line is not the shortest distance between two points," says Mrs. Whatsit, an astral being who guides the children in their interstellar journey.[3] It is Mrs. Whatsit who introduces the children to tesseract time travel. In a pivotal passage, Mrs. Whatsit likens tessering to an ant crawling across a skirt. The ant can take "the long way," marching straight across from point A to point B, *or*—she pinches the skirt to connect the two points—

the ant could simply take a shortcut across the fabric fold. This "wrinkle" is the tesser: a shortcut.

To be alive is to move through time and space. So surely we are constantly tessering—but not always tessering well. Mostly, we'd prefer to tesser *out of* unpleasant times and spaces, and tesser only *into* brighter, happier, more successful, more settled times. But that's not how life works. Life holds a startlingly diverse array of experiences, and we do not get to choose the time we're in.

Contrary to the hero's journey, which suggests time is only well spent toward rising success, the Scriptures say otherwise. There is a time for everything, we are told, a season for everything under the sun: "a time to be born and a time to die, a time to plant and a time to uproot" (Ecclesiastes 3:2). A time to weep, laugh, mourn, and dance. "A time to scatter stones and a time to gather them" (Ecclesiastes 3:5).[4]

And so the circle turns, again and again and again.

The heart of the triquetra, the womb of God, the liturgical year—it seems to me that tessering might be simply the way we move around the circle of time. Maybe this is the essence of taking on the risks of life and love: accepting that there is a time for everything, and trusting that God is with us, around the circle, in every time. God with us in the birthing, the dying, the weeping, the gathering. God with us in mothers wailing and prophets rejoicing. God with us in every experience of love, loss, and liminality.

L'Engle describes tessering as traveling at faster than the speed of light. One might say that tessering is traveling at the speed of love—a love that never lets go, no matter what dimension we find ourselves in.

Sacred time is the tesseract by which divine love breaks into our here and now, wrinkling the hem of eternity to be *with us*, traveling through space and time to be with the beloved. The li-

turgical year is not about memorializing the past; it's a living remembrance that reaches into our here and now, as if to take our
hand and say: *Here, trace the pattern. Feel the deep grooves of motion
across time, the center that will hold, the pattern that will not break.*

Maybe the invitation is not to shut down, retreat from all risk,
or one-dimensionally "overcome," but to go around the circle
ever deepening and drawing closer to the beating heart of love
itself.

Maybe this is the heart of authentic resilience—not muscling
through the "After," but learning to stay in the tension, trusting
God-with-us, and so cultivating the kind of strength that is able
to sustain us around the circle again.

In the "After" of any hardship, I have found two things to be of
great support. Community: who is with us. And genesis: where
and who we come from. The word "genealogy" speaks to both.

Mary had a deep understanding of her place within her long
line of kin, both ancient and future, heralded on high display as
she sang in her Magnificat: "From now on all generations will
call me blessed" (Luke 1:48). Her song speaks of the Messiah as
the fulfillment of a promise made to ancient ancestors as it cas-
cades through future generations, to their descendants forever.

I wonder if this wider view is what might have sustained her
as the prophet spoke of her future pain.

And I wonder if we might source a similar strength through
looking beyond our individual hardships in the wider view of our
collective genealogical wisdom and resilience.

When Hurricane Harvey slammed Houston in 2017, it sub-
merged large swaths of the city underwater, and an elderly man
was trapped in his car in the rising flood. Neighbors who probably didn't even know each others' names gripped hand to hand
in a chest-high current, forming a human chain to bring him to

safety, and the story went national as people resonated with this profound act of humanity in desperate circumstances.

There are so many ways to find yourself underwater. But what I know for sure is that none of us are meant to carry the weight of this life alone. Here's what I think we've gotten wrong about resilience: It is not the feather in the cap of the hero's journey, because it is not a solo journey at all. Rather, authentic resilience can only be a communal practice. We are meant to carry each other. We are meant to be carried by thinking-of-you texts, dinner drop-offs, friends and family who keep vigil with us, remember hard dates year after year, take us to the movies when we don't feel like talking.

And perhaps one of the most profound remembrances of this is found in our very biology.

Your earliest biological beginning traces back to your maternal grandmother's womb. As early as twenty weeks in utero, a female fetus has developed ovaries with a lifetime supply of eggs. The implications of this are nothing less than sacred, as it means there was a time in your grandmother's pregnancy when she carried not just your mother, but also the earliest part of you. Her body, in this precise tesser of time, was haven to three generations—so long a future, tightly intertwined within.

Our stories began in so humble a shimmer, couplets of cells in sleeping prologue for—think of it—a quarter or a third of a lifetime. I think of those inaugural atoms, patient as the ancient earth, but even then, a whispered beginning.

Trace this biological connection back and back and back, daughter to mother to grandmother, matriarch to matriarch, and you will find your maternal line. Trace it all the way back to the beginning, if you like, to the original woman, who once walked with God. And you will find it is something akin to a human chain.

Perhaps when you consider your maternal line you see legacy, wisdom, and other gifts being passed downstream. Or perhaps you do not see this at all, but rather a trauma-laden, frictioned heritage you'd rather not be in biological communion with. Or maybe yours is a swerving inheritance, one that veers between gifts and burdens. Yet I have to think somewhere along the long way of women before us there is love, and great hope and good-will given toward future generations, which includes you and me.

In hurricane season, human chains save lives. And in swell seasons of personal struggle, the anchor of ancestral love can keep us steady amid any churning current. Reaching across borders of time, space, and memory, our matriarchs hold hands through generations, and we are held by them. And as we join hands into the chain ourselves, we strand the powers of our being together and create a line, bright and unbreakable, slicing through the dark expanse. As Parker Palmer writes, "We are participants in a vast communion of being."[5]

In a flood, off the frothing coast, people form a human chain often because they don't have a rope for rescue, but we do. Our mothers fought with their very bodies for us to be here, and when we arrived, tied a knot at our center, secure as a sailor's. Look, lift up your shirt and see, we give it a name that makes children giggle, but it is the body's first scar, sealing our belonging. It is a sign and sacrament of the cord that once tethered you to your mother and her mother and all her mothers before, and in this collective love and wisdom, you are tethered still. You and I are here because we have been carried, however imperfectly.

For all the ways we might feel free-floating and alone, and for all the generational ills and trauma, I have to believe there are gifts for us somewhere along this line, especially the further back we trace it. Our ancestral memory is surely a sacred trust, extending to us today centuries of wisdom and resilience that are far beyond our years.

The tides of life may swell, the depths may overwhelm, but we remain held by the human chain that is our matriarchal line, reaching all the way back to our first mother in the garden, when God said, *She is good.* We are that which the serpent must contend with. We, the cosmic force that shall crush the head. We, the warriors of the last word. This cloud of witnesses longs to mother us, should we let it. We are held in the human chain of our mothers, and they are held by the womb of God, the Mother of us all. Surely, when crisis comes, we have great reserves of resilience to draw from, strength borrowing strength.

When I was a newborn, my mother's mother was a new widow. She lost a husband—the redheaded love of her life who could always make her laugh—and gained a granddaughter all in the span of a few weeks. In labor, my mother cried two rivers: one for the father who was impossibly gone, one for the daughter who was blessedly now here.

A stroke. A swaddling cloth. A cradle. A casket. Water breaking, in so many directions. This is how I came into the world. We all needed to be held, then—my mother, her mother, and me. And we were—even in so much grief, the love held and held.

Overcoming is an individualist project, but I cannot believe resilience is all on us, nor that it was ever meant to be. I think of my mother and her mother and my great-grandmother, this maternal line, who passed their lifeblood and love to a little one we will never hold yet love forever. I consider this cloud of witnesses, and some ancient grace floated out to me, like a rope upon the waves. It is an old support, threaded through generations, and now that it had come to me, I held it fast.

5

REMEMBERING YOUR DEATH, TRYING FOR LIFE

Ash Wednesday and Lent

I AM the embodied God
With You in the full seasons of your humanity, even
  death

Though terrors surely await us, we take our chances that—
all things considered—life is worth living.

JERRY SITTSER, "Life after Loss"

I used to joke that Ash Wednesday is the high holiday of Enneagram fours, we who feel strangely more at home in the minor keys, who are consoled by meditations of mortality because to us they tell the truth.

I don't make that joke anymore.

Lent is a layered season, with ancient echoes. It is a season marked by dust and ashes, giving up and going without, the purple cloth of penitence draped over the altar and the cross.

Its forty days stretch from Ash Wednesday to Easter Sunday—
not counting Sunday "feast days"—echoing Jesus' forty days in

the desert during which he faced his temptations, and the Israelites' forty years in the wilderness before that.

And it begins with ashes: the anointing no one ever asked for. Ashes are all that's left after the burning, after the scorched earth, after our hope has become the burned-over district. Who would ever ask for that? I suppose this is why the liturgy calls it an imposition.

"Remember that you are dust, and to dust you will return," leads the Lenten liturgy as the ashes are crossed on our foreheads. This tradition is long, tracing back to the fifth century, early Middle Ages, refraining a heartbroken God's words to the first humans after they chose death for themselves.

Ash Wednesday marks the start of a somber season, though I have no interest in Lent purely as self-abnegation. I have too often seen and participated myself in Lent as fixating on some sense of personalized wretchedness, which can too easily slip into attempts to earn God's favor. What's more, it must be recognized that Lent expresses a human condition, and for many of us, the experience of Lent is not a time-bound season we can opt in and out of at will, but an unbroken reality offering no relief. Life is burdened by many long Lents that don't let up just because the calendar has crossed over Easter Sunday. For those of us who experience chronic illness or discrimination against the bodies in which we live, forgoing Lenten fasting for self-nourishment might make for a more meaningful spiritual practice. For those of us who are working through past trauma, observing Lent might mean repenting of the injustices we have participated in, even as we recount and recover from the injustices that have caused us harm.

If Ash Wednesday is a somber season, it is so in the way that it is a clear-eyed coming to terms. It is a reckoning with the real. "The moment you are born you begin dying," writes Sister Theresa Aletheia Noble. "You may die in ten years, fifty years, perhaps tomorrow—or even today. But whenever it happens, death awaits every person."[1]

We know our end. Yet why do we so rarely engage this ultimate reality?

Lent need not be sin dramatized or penance performed; it is enough to make the simple, self-aware confession of all we are not: infallible, in control, immortal. It is enough to name the pain we have suffered and own the ways we have participated in the pain of others. Ash Wednesday has a way of cutting through the hubris, the ego and pretense of all that my friend Seth Haines calls "The Show," and this can be profoundly, counterintuitively revitalizing.[2] Ash Wednesday might be for us a sort of near-death experience, waking us up to the profound gift of living this singular life.

Nadia Bolz-Weber writes, "If our lives were a long piece of fabric with our baptism on one end and our funeral on another, and we don't know the distance between the two, then Ash Wednesday is a time when that fabric is pinched in the middle and the ends are held up so that our baptism in the past and our funeral in the future meet. . . . And in that meeting we are reminded of the promises of God: That we are God's, that there is no sin, no darkness, and yes, no grave that God will not come to find us in and love us back to life. These promises outlast our earthly bodies and the limits of time."[3]

Nadia does not use this word, but the image she creates so precisely here is to me a tesser: a wrinkling of time. On Ash Wednesday, we become time travelers, ants on the hem, the length of our lives pinched and pleated to reveal our end. And in that end, we find an invitation. Ash Wednesday is not here to say our lives don't matter, given the end. It's here to say this life, this enfleshed, dirt-under-the-fingernails life, is undeniably sacred.

We remember our death not to lie down and accept our fate, but to stand up and live in full presence the life that we have.

The truth is that our bodies are in the process of returning to dust all the time, even as we live. The dust we sweep out of the corners of our homes, that children swipe fingers through on the window-sills, is an original composition of many things, including, yes, our skin cells. Our bodies hold two concurrent stories ever in conversation: the story of decay, of shedding cells, of returning to dust, and also the story of regeneration—letting go to make way for the new.

What is dust? Particle-proof of a world falling apart. Dead skin cells, once-golden pollen now in decay, the ash of ancient volcanoes, salt crystals stranded from the sea, minerals ground down by wind and time. All of it—tiny fossils of what once was, blown by the wind.

What is dust? Evidence of entropy. Dust tells the story of what was, what has since fallen apart.

This is true of not only our particular bodies, but the cosmic body, as well. Each year, one billion metric tons of mineral dust from the earth's driest regions are windswept through the atmosphere.[4] This volume is so significant that NASA tracks it, seeking to understand its atmospheric heating and cooling properties. Mineral dust is powerful for being so particle small—it can enhance the colors of a sunset, act as nutrient-rich fertilizer as it falls on forests and oceans, prompting large-scale plankton blooms, and influence cloud formation and rainfall.

Even so, it is the inevitability of dust to sift low, to return to still life like sand in the hourglass. Maybe that's why we try so hard to sweep it away from the places in which we live, sweeping away the suggestion of our mortality with it. Maybe that's why we expend so much energy denying death, in what Pulitzer Prize–winning anthropologist Ernest Becker names our "primary repression."[5]

When presented as our end, dust seems a humble thing. Yet when it is reconsidered as our origin story, as well, it awakens wonder. As astronomer Carl Sagan famously observed, "We are made of star stuff."[6] But how can this be? At first blush, it sounds like a stretch, a fringe theory perhaps, yet this is a face-value, unquestioned baseline among much of the scientific community.

Here's what we know.

Most of the elements in the human body were first formed inside of stars, and we know this because these raw elements of life don't originate anywhere else in the universe.

The core of a star is like a furnace, heating and pressuring atoms so intensely that they begin to fuse together, forming new elements. When a star has burned through all its fuel, it explodes in what is called a nova or a supernova, releasing these original elements into the cosmos as stardust. And these elements are the basis for all organic life on earth.

At the most basic biological level, humankind shares 97 percent of the same atomic matter as our galaxy.[7]

Every molecule of oxygen in our lungs, carbon in our muscles, calcium in our bones, iron in our blood, nitrogen in our DNA finds its ultimate origin in the life of an ancient star. For as vast as the universe is and as small as we sometimes feel in it, we share an exquisite intimacy with the cosmos.

How I imagine it: Supernovas flame the ancient sky, their stardust falling like a first snow, anointing the earth of Eden, integrating with the soil that kissed the knees of a kneeling God. In the garden of our beginning, God cupped hands to the earth, lifted an open palm of stardust-flecked soil, and breathed. *Let there be life,* exhaled the I AM, and our being began.

Wendell Berry once wrote that the soil "is the great connector of lives, the source and destination of all."[8] Perhaps this connection runs deeper than we know. Dust to dust is the journey of a life, as Ash Wednesday reminds us. This is the story, its beginning and its end. Yet maybe it's not so morose as we might first think. After all, these ashes speak two truths:

We are dust; we are stardust.

We are soil; we are interstellar.

We are ants on a hem, mere dust particles on Sagan's pale blue dot, which is to say we are mortal. We are also imago Dei, containing the multitudes of God and galaxies.

And in these ashes even now, galaxies still swirl.[9]

I went to the Ash Wednesday service alone that year. Zach had left on an early flight that morning to head to a campus job interview, so I walked myself in and found a seat at the back. The sanctuary was bare, stripped down to spare oak, save for the purple cloth on the otherwise empty altar. Outside, the sun was setting. We began the liturgy in the blue hour.

I knelt to receive the imposition of ashes, but I did not need to be prompted to remember my death. I had already experienced death in my own body, and it would never forget. An intimate part of me had already returned to the dust.

A family filed in behind me and there was a baby with perfect lashes waving a tiny plush giraffe. I looked away when the ashes came to her.

A change had taken place in me. I had not begun the journey of "trying" with desire. There had been no heat of *want* at the beginning, only a cognitive recognition that our vision for the future included a family, and trust in that even if the emotions weren't there. But now, on the other side of loss, ashes on my brow, I was unnerved by the power of it: *want*. There were no qualifiers, no caveats, no asterisked disclaimers—grief had trans-figured all of that into raw, barreling clarity.

I felt it now with a fire. It was precisely remembering my death that made me want to try for life.

And I had been trying, starting with the healing of my body. It became clear to me that my body, post-miscarriage, had been going through a hard reset. And I wanted to give her generous space to recover, as well as take the time to listen to and learn from her as perhaps I never had before. So I had started the new year with a personal reading and research list about hormonal health for women.

When I first got my period, the first person I told was my mom—and I still remember the way she threw up her hands and danced around the kitchen, her joy giving liberative wing to mine. She took me out to lunch that very day to celebrate—"*You're a woman now*"—and it felt beautiful: a sacred beginning. But it wasn't long before I caught wind of other narratives. When I told my best friend the news, I assured her we'd celebrate when her time came, too. Then I learned it already had, some time ago—and she'd never told me.

All that joy skidded into the hard stop: *Oh—some things are meant to be unspoken.* Teachers and youth leaders affirmed this by speaking about our menstruation in code, skirting direct refer-ences with air quotes and sidelong winks that made it plain: *We don't talk about this, not even among ourselves.*

My body was commencing a new kind of becoming, which was always meant to be beautiful, and for a moment, it was. But then shame clipped the wings of joy.

For many years afterward, as it is for many women, my cycle became a monthly inconvenience, a flat fact of logistics to man-age, though I didn't even always do this well.

Once in the early years of our marriage, in a particular era of prolonged overwork and burnout, I went nearly six months without a period. But the worst part is, my body was breaking the glass and sounding the alarm, yet I was too preoccupied to hear her distress signals. The saddest thing to me about this is that it never occurred to me to seek medical help or start asking questions. It never occurred to me—not once—to take a pregnancy test, just to be certain.

One of the books I read summed up this shame narrative as the predominant belief that "female hormones were messy and problematic, something that needed to be 'fixed.' Menstruation and menopause were considered embarrassing topics. . . . There was 'the curse,' there was 'the change,' and in between there were the shadowy topics of sex, pregnancy, and childbirth."[10]

For much of my life, I had felt as so many women do: that my period was something that *held me back* from my actual life. It was a disruption, defined by sick days and sitting the pool out and staying home with a heating pad. The way I saw it, my period was essentially punitive, removing me from my life in some kind of biological time-out.

But I was just now discovering that the medical community had a radically different name for what I was calling a problem to manage. They called it the fifth vital sign, elevating menstrual health to the essential functions of body temperature, blood pressure, heart rate, and breathing rate.[11] What I saw as a liability was actually an embodied icon of life itself. What I saw as an inconvenience was actually the wisdom of the body at work, a somatic intelligence that I had sidelined and silenced for far too long.

Well before I developed a certain squeamishness toward the embodied acts of pregnancy and parenting, I realized, I had already taken the stance that my cycle was just a grimy reality standing between me and the life I thought I wanted. Now, upon closer inspection, this was not the relationship with my body that

I wanted, nor the life. This squeamishness is learned, spoken into our lives by the tale as old as time that women should be sorry for taking up space; that we should apologize by making ourselves small and keeping our messy, bodily realities out of sight. My work was now unlearning the ways I had been taught to disdain the life of the body, particularly the life of a woman's body.

Our bodies are our primary way of being in the world, so when we neglect its needs, we experience estrangement in our most intimate relationship. Philosopher Charles Taylor has a striking name for this sidelining of the body. He calls it "excarnation": "the steady disembodying of spiritual life, so that it is less and less carried in deeply meaningful bodily forms, and lies more and more in the head."[12]

In Taylor's description, excarnation is the consequence of exalting the life of the mind over the life of the body. But surely excarnation can have varying expressions, as one exalts image, ambition and success, or digital life to the detriment and displacement of our bodies. Excarnation might look like squashing down hunger pangs or a gut feeling, over-caffeinating to compensate for last night's deadline push or late night out, or outsourcing our lives to screens so much that it changes our spinal structure. It might look like belittling the intensely embodied work of motherhood, an insidious impulse I was only just beginning to recognize in myself.

If the Incarnation speaks of the word made flesh, excarnation expresses in the denial of bodily needs, and at its utmost, the denial of the body's inevitable end in death. If the Incarnation narrates the full life cycle through life, death, and ultimate resurrection, excarnation insists on life as one immortal summer, eyes shut to the creaturely realities of change, aging, and dying.

I had practiced excarnation for too long. For all the ways I had silenced the life of the body, I was ready to listen. I had a lot to learn, as well as unlearn. And my discoveries began with the recognition that I had reduced the concept of my cycle to merely the period part of it, when in reality, a woman's cycle moves through a vibrant spectrum of inner seasons.

Most of us have heard of the circadian rhythm, the body's baseline wake-to-sleep cycle within a twenty-four-hour period. The circadian rhythm regulates our basic biological functions such as sleep, digestion, metabolism, and the production of hormones, which for all their stigma are simply chemical signals sent through the bloodstream from one part of the body to another. For women and men alike, the circadian rhythm sets the tempo for our daily patterns, sunrise to sunset.

Women, however, have another cycle at work. For women, the daily circadian rhythm is overlaid with a second rhythm unique to them from puberty through menopause. The infradian rhythm is comprised of four distinct hormonal stages that the body will cycle through in an average of twenty-eight days, or one month. And in this infradian rhythm, we find an invitation to what has been called cycle syncing: the practice of turning our attention toward our embodied rhythms so we might live within them with greater intention.[13]

Cycle syncing takes a partnership perspective toward our bodies instead of a problem-management perspective. Instead of fighting against our body's natural rhythms, resenting its needs, or pushing it to be at perpetual peak, cycle syncing allows for the full expanse of our hormonal ebbs and flows, so we might live at peace within every phase of the cycle.

While the circadian and infradian rhythms are commonly referred to as biological clocks, this strikes me as too mechanical for something so complex and mysterious. I much prefer the metaphor of inner seasons, as one natural cycle mirrors another. The seasons metaphor also casts a more inclusive vision of cycle syncing, as inner spring, summer, fall, and winters can be experienced by everyone—regardless of biology, life stage, birth control choices, or self-identification.[14]

The follicular stage, or preovulatory stage, is often likened to an inner spring. It is a season of growth, as the estrogen hormone rises and the uterus thickens to prepare for a potential egg to implant and grow. This season is marked by possibility and momentum, reflective of the new blooms and beginnings of spring.[15] Women report an upswing in creative and social energy during the follicular stage, perhaps mirroring the generative, outward focus of what's happening biologically.[16]

When estrogen reaches its threshold point, this becomes the brain's signal to produce the luteinizing hormone, which then spikes rapidly and signals to the ovaries that it's time to release an egg. This ovulation stage is the peak of fertility, in an expression of inner summer.

And, like summer, this is a season that naturally draws us to be *out* in the world. It is a season of opening and reaching outward, commonly marked by felt vitality, confidence, and human connection. Women report high self-esteem at this point in their cycle.[17] The energy that was on an upswing during the follicular stage is now at its peak.

In the luteal phase, both estrogen and the luteinizing hormone experience a dramatic drop-off, and progesterone rises in their place, causing the uterine lining to prepare for a possible implantation. While estrogen has an energizing effect, progesterone has a powerful calming effect on the nervous system, bringing equilibrium to anxiety and inflammation, promoting sleep, and naturally drawing a person inward. The body in the luteal phase tends to slow down, perhaps because it is working to pay close attention to whether this cycle will result in a pregnancy or not.

This phase might be seen as an inner fall: a time for slowing the pace, closing loops, and bringing things into completion, all in preparation for the coming winter.

The luteal phase is also the period in which many women experience the symptoms of premenstrual syndrome (PMS), such as bloating, cramping, breast tenderness, and mood changes. I was surprised to learn that such symptoms, while common, are not normative. Rather, they are our body's signals that there is a hormonal imbalance that needs tending to. The silencing effect of stigma and the ingrained expectation that monthly suffering is "just part of being a woman" create a dangerous imperative when they converge, and the imperative is clear: *Endure in silence. Your pain is not socially acceptable; keep it to yourself.*

If any of our other vital signs were acting up—temperatures breaking a hundred, irregular breathing—no one would say, "Well, it's just part of being human." We would get seen. We would receive care. Yet half of the global population has been commonly conditioned to suffer in silence when one of their vital signs starts shouting distress signals.

Finally, the luteal gives way to the menstrual phase.

When the body discerns there is no new pregnancy to support, both progesterone and estrogen levels decline until reaching their lowest points in the cycle, and this prompts the uterine lining to let go and start the menstrual flow. The day your period begins is technically day one of a new cycle, though it can help to understand the full lead-up. The greatest need during the menstrual phase is rest, as the body experiences blood loss and the energy depletion that accompanies this.

This inner winter is a time to draw inward, leaning into rest and renewal. Such retreat is intentional and designed to be deeply restorative, as we trade collaborative work for deep work, and social connection for contemplative quiet. During the menstrual phase, the creative right and logical left brain are in deeper communication than any other time during the cycle, so this is an excellent time to get quiet and check in with yourself, look for new connections, and listen to your intuition.[18]

What I love about this portrait of inner seasons is their range—the way they suggest, much like the liturgical seasons, that there is a right time for everything. As Katherine May writes in *Wintering,* "We like to imagine that it's possible for life to be one eternal summer. . . . We dream of an equatorial habitat, forever close to the sun; an endless, unvarying high season. But life's not like that."[19]

And we need not shame ourselves into pretending that it is. As much as productivity culture glorifies it, none of us are meant for full capacity all the time. Summer is not perpetual and we are not immortal. Rather, we find our deepest life in accepting the full range itself, each of its varying experiences in their time.

The liturgical cycle tells the story of the Incarnation: God becoming human and living out the full seasons and physical senses of the human experience—inhabiting all, bypassing none. Living out our interior seasons with intention can be a profound practice of incarnation, one that dignifies the body's needs and natural cycles, while excarnation denies them. One that learns to listen to the physical senses as they speak to us, for they are always speaking.

It was pregnancy loss and hope for pregnancy that prompted me to understand my cycle in new ways, yet cycle syncing is wisdom that carries into every area of life—regardless of partnership or parenthood status. My only regret was that I did not come into this wisdom sooner. While a woman's cycle is biologically based in reproduction, out of all the cycles we experience in a lifetime, only a few if any will progress into a pregnancy. Yet cycle awareness is undoubtedly about creating life—first and foremost, *your own*. It is the generative practice of living out your inner liturgy with intention. It is indeed the practice of creating a life, one that spans the inner seasons and all their gifts.

Living within the liturgy of one's cycle not only supports the process of trying for or preventing pregnancy, it can bring greater alignment between our physical and psychological health for whole-person benefits. And ultimately, such alignment can be deeply angst saving. Instead of berating our energy drops during our luteal stage, we can be at peace knowing that our body is downshifting and now is not the time to push hard. Instead of racking ourselves with "What's wrong with me?" cycle syncing can help us accept the inner season we're in, *knowing* that it is temporary yet also for the time being it is *right* and the body's wisdom at work.

Cycle awareness and its benefits may be brought to our eating and exercise patterns, our workflow and creative projects, our social life and self-care practices. Mainly, knowing where you are in your cycle can help you accept your capacity and manage your energy in the way your body most needs. I don't believe cycle syncing is meant to be a grid—just another fixed binary of "good" and "bad" choices—but rather a lived poetry as we learn to listen to our innermost needs.

For the first time in my life, I was waking up to the power of my biology, as hormonal health researcher and author Alisa Vitti puts it. In my own inner season of winter, sustaining our loss and the powerlessness that accompanied it, I felt this new understanding for what it was: a reclamation.

What's more, by reclaiming the sacred dimensions of my cycle, I was also being awakened to the sacred dimensions of pregnancy, birth, and motherhood. Where I had once regarded this realm as basic and reductive, I could no longer deny their profound depths and mysteries. And I have no other way to think about it than as a mystery. Surely there is great agency in the choice to live within our given rhythms, yet there is also great surrender in the choice to try for new life. To try to conceive, one must endure a cascade of surrenders: first, the outcome of such an effort, the shape of a life as it is altered by this singular exchange of care, and any knowledge or control over just who this new person might be or become. And surrender will always be the site of transformation.

We might say that a woman's body is in orbit.

A woman's body tells the story of the world, the story of the cosmos, the very story God has been singing from the start: one of radical birth and rebirth. Twelve times each year, her body "move[s] rhythmically through a creation cycle."[20]

I might add that twelve times each year, her body moves through a Paschal cycle, tracing in the ancient pattern of life, death, and resurrection. This Paschal rhythm runs like a river through her bloodstream, proclaiming the mystery beneath all mysteries: not only life, but life that usurps death. Her very circulation pulses with the ancient-present promise: We will rise again. Surely a woman who lives her days in touch with this elemental truth is a woman greatly alive.

Just as the liturgical circle holds space for the full spectrum of our humanity, so does the lived liturgy of a woman's body through her menstrual cycle. In this sacred orbit, everything belongs—the revitalizing possibilities of spring, the bright energy of summer, the fresh winds and focused drive of fall, the restorative retreat of winter. Through every season, her body is a temple—that much does not change. And the very creation story God loves to tell finds its symmetry in her. The ancient powers of beginning are embedded in her being. Every turn of the moon is another genesis, another chance at making a life, starting with her own.

She is wise, then, to accept such astonishing range as somatic intelligence designed to sustain and enliven, and not as a liability meant to limit.

Human civilizations have long recognized the parallels between the natural cycles of the earth and the fertility cycles of women, as reflected across the traditions and rituals of many ancient cultures. The earth and its circle of seasons is not unlike a womb, and we are participants in this cycle, in an integral, embodied way.

Yet sacred time infuses this familiar cycle with new dimension, because the Paschal cycle does not ask us to repeat life to death ad infinitum. Rather, the Paschal cycle invites us to inhabit the seasons of life and death *until* it ultimately gives way to resurrection. This is a cycle that completes itself not in death, but in life.

Hope is embedded in the cycle of seasons: Spring will come again. But the Christian hope runs even deeper: Ultimately, spring will come to *stay*. We are not asked to trust the cycling of the seasons simply because it is the natural way of things. Our trust is grounded in the assurance that reality itself—everything we consider "natural" now—will be re-storied by resurrection. We can endure the dust, the ashes, the inner winters, because resurrection as the final reality, the last word on all mortal seasons and cycles, can be trusted. While dust to dust might be the pattern for now, we can find our courage in knowing that when God breathes into the dust, it comes to life again, and this time, life endures.

We are culturally catechized to excarnation, ingrained in the illusion that the body is second to ego and image, that perpetual summer and happiness might be achieved if we hustle hard enough, that death might come for others but not for us. When the body is seen only as an impediment to aspired immortality, trying to escape the natural cycles—of our bodies, of the seasons, of life to death—becomes an urgent task. At its utmost, excarnation is simply escapism.

Yet the reality of resurrection gives us the courage we need to fully incarnate our mortal bodies here and now, in the knowledge that Paschal death is passage to life upon life. With this wider view, we can inhabit the cycle of seasons now in the confidence that it will lead to resurrection, which is where incarnation always leads.

I had given myself the winter to heal. But now we were turning into early spring, and we had a decision to make. My mom and therapist seemed to feel it would be wise to wait, given the coronavirus concerns. My doctor didn't advise on it exactly, but cited that fertility clinics nationwide were temporarily halting any new IVF treatments. The case was a simple one: "What's two months?" betraying the depth of our early optimism that this virus spike would all go away in a measurable amount of time. That was back when there was speculation about a "second wave" coming rather than a sprawling, endless expanse of sickness and risk and exposure.

The question of trying was no longer a hypothetical. We had to get honest with ourselves: Is this the kind of world we want to bring a child into?

I read an essay by a woman who was wrestling with this very question in the same global moment. I highlighted one of her final lines: "To decide to have children is, after all, to take a stance on one of the most fundamental questions a person can ask: Is human life, despite all the suffering and uncertainty it entails, worth living?"[21]

Someone tagged me in a photo on Facebook from a publishing panel I had spoken on just a few months before everything shut down. In the photo, I am sitting high on a stool, crossing my legs in my block heels and silk shirt dress, mic in one hand and talking with the other. I look like a woman at ease with herself, yet I remembered with a twist. In this still life frame, there was life still. I hadn't known it then, though I had felt bloated that weekend. But this is what stayed with me: When I looked at her, and considered the mystery then within me, I felt love rise up. And it was rising still.

Poet Billy Ray Belcourt writes, "To love someone is firstly to confess: I am prepared to be devastated by you."[22] I had known devastation. And now, even in the aftershocks, I was getting to know desire. And with it, maybe even hope.

Ultimately, if this—if anything—is a love story, it is a risk story. This is the choice, this is the confession: To open ourselves to love is to consent to the kingdom of infinity-flung contingencies. Nothing is more vulnerable than this choice. And yet, nothing is more meaningful.

What a different world ours would be if God, after all things considered, elected *not* to create life that may or may not love in return, that might even choose death for themselves. If God had left our future entirely a hypothetical question, something from a distant dream. Instead, God made himself vulnerable to devastation. Rather than confining communion to within the Trinity— a closed circle forever—God loosed the world open to love and all its contingencies. God said yes anyway, and breathed this divine yes into our lungs, giving us being and setting the whole story in motion. We are here because God—for all love, and against all risks—decided for life, in defiance of death.

My friend Roxy had been married for ten years when her husband took her to dinner on a weeknight and told her he didn't want to be married anymore. No one had seen this coming, least of all her, and here it was—a sudden death. Ten years, crumbled to dust.

Some years later—after some hard-won healing, after a cross-coastal move for a long-distance boyfriend, after months of pre-marital counseling and ring browsing, so much fresh hope and energy to turn a new page—the boyfriend called her while she was on an international trip. In twenty minutes, it was over. He never gave her a reason. They never spoke again.

How do you trust after trust has been broken and broken? The self-preservationist in all of us says, *Better not to trust at all. Better not to try.*

It took time, therapy, no small acts of God, and a friend saying *there's someone we think you should meet* before she was willing to take that risk again. His name was John, and the more she got to know him, the more she wanted to. There was more premarital counseling, more ring talk, more risk. From the outside, it might have looked like a setup, some dark déjà vu.

But this time, my friend decided to risk on her own terms.

Roxy's dad had just died suddenly of a heart attack, and in her shock and grief, John kept showing up for her, as their relationship took on new depths. He flew out to meet her and her mom in Colorado, and they decided to take in the great West, creating space for her to process and remember, before going back to New York City where they lived.

They were hiking in the Grand Canyon, standing on the seeming edge of the world, when she gave him a diamond. She voiced one of the riskiest questions any of us can ask, with all its contingent vulnerability: Would you make a life, a future with me, for whatever it might hold?

If this is a love story, it is a risk story.

The diamond was a family heirloom, and John would select a second diamond to accompany it in the same setting so he could propose to her in turn. This way, they both got to say yes.

I love the story her ring tells. Two stones in equal weight, joined together. A call and a response. A question risked and re-ciprocated.

Madeleine L'Engle once told the story of reviewing a screen-play proposal for *A Wrinkle in Time*. She opened the first page, and closed it again. "He doesn't get it," she told her agent. Had he even read the book?

The screenwriter had written a three-word epigraph to start the work: "Love is power."

"Love is not power," L'Engle wrote in rejoinder. "Love is giv-ing power away. Power in the sense of control."[23]

Choosing to trust again, try again, is never a blank slate sce-nario. The history of our hurt is just as layered as fossil-rich can-yon rock—the story of millions of years of geological formation as told in the strata.

So, no, love is not power. Love is standing on the edge of a canyon deep with your heart in your hands, saying, *Of all the people in the world, you could hurt me the most, and yet because I love you, will you have me?*

It is fitting that we remember our death in our marriage vows—*till death do us part*—acknowledging the end even as we begin. But it doesn't keep us from living.

Perhaps love, in its truest form, takes the shape of surrender. Love is a downright requiem of control. That's precisely what makes love so daring. That's what makes love's trying so brave.

I went to the Ash Wednesday service alone that year. I knelt to receive the imposition of ashes. I looked away when the ashes came to the baby.

But even as we remembered our death, I was holding a secret, a new hope in my heart. That morning well before the sun came up and Zach caught his early flight to his interview, I had reached for him. This trip had been a source of stress for my cycle, our hopes, our limited window. On this day of memento mori, it was a decision made of defiance. Against the forces of death, it was a decision to try.

If we look closely, this very sacred subversion stirs in the ashes even now.

My friend Ken is a priest and a chaplain for the sheriff's office in Detroit. He has seen much of death. He's the one they call to come for the loved ones who have lost their son, brother, sister to an overdose. He's the one who is there to restrain from self-harm the weeping parents whose child won't be coming home after a school shooting.

And so I trust it deeply when he says, "The good news of Ash Wednesday is that when the human God dies, death itself begins to work backwards."

There is only one who did not—will not—return to dust. And his life sets into motion a subversion that will disrupt death forever. It stirred my courage to know that even these ashes hold the origin story of galaxies, just as they hold the future glimmers of resurrection. Maybe this is why we consider Lent to be a season of "bright sadness."[24]

While it may seem counterintuitive, I have come to believe Ash Wednesday frees us to practice incarnation, because incarnation will always lead to resurrection. The body of God will always lead our bodies—through the soil, the ashes, through every natural cycle—to life that lasts and lasts.

6

RECEIVING THE JOY

Holy Week and Easter

I AM the good you can believe
With You in the vulnerability of joy

It takes practice to face the reality of darkness, but also to
ask for—and hope for—light.

TISH HARRISON WARREN, *Prayer in the Night*

It was springtime, Lent was leaning toward Easter, and I was
obsessed with signs of life. While my Ash Wednesday hopes
had not been fulfilled, I was still listening keenly to my body,
tracking its cycle, and trying to honor its rhythms.

I hardly recognized myself. I'd never done this before, the
hope part, the *want* part, of trying. Never walked through the
electric anxiety of the two-week wait. The obsessive caliber reminded me of high school crushes, what it's like to replay every
syllable, sifting through every interaction for signals, meaning.
Only now I turned this toward the mystery of my own body:
Was this an early symptom? Was this a sign, or just stress? Meanwhile, in these early days of quarantine, Zach and I were each
privately googling Covid symptoms, so as not to frighten the
other. Our search histories could tell quite a story.

I entered Holy Week much like the disciples: with high hopes.

Holy Week is a week of superlative emotions. This week in the sacred year might be understood as a microcosm of the human experience, moving from the highest hopes to deepest disappointment to the worst kind of waiting to vibrant joy.

On Palm Sunday, Jesus rides into Jerusalem as if a king, surely the king all of Israel had been waiting for! But then, on Maundy Thursday, Jesus kneels to wash the feet of his students in a rather un-king-like way, then rattles all their nerves by talking about his death. "Remember me," he tells them, breaking the bread and passing the wine, in the most ominous meal he's shared with his disciples yet.

Then on Good Friday, the unthinkable happens. Hope had become human, and then this human takes a final breath. Imagine it: The heart that set the story of the world in motion, the heart that sent all others beating, flatlines—for the first time in the history of time.

The emptiness of this day is echoed visually in a stripped altar—no cloth, no color, no flowers. Some churches lead a Tenebrae service—a Latin word for "darkness" or "shadows"—which follows the passion of Christ through a series of readings. As the story progresses, the candles are extinguished, one by one, in a slow-motion descent into darkness. And the usual alleluias of the liturgy are absent, in the tradition of "burying the alleluias" during Lent. Because now is not the time for celebration, but for lament.

I had certainly buried the alleluias. My womb had become an altar stripped. I had known lament.

Tori Amos once said in an interview about her experience of miscarriage, "Once you've felt life in your body, you can't go back to having been a woman that's never carried life. [You are] feeling something dying inside of you and you're still alive."[1]

As I entered Holy Week that year, I considered this: The living God remembers what it is like to die. My body is a place where life was wanted, but where death has happened. There is no greater schism than life and death, and every woman who has experienced pregnancy loss endures so great a divide in her very body.

How wild it is to think Christ knows what this deep divide is like. The body of Christ holds the scars, the somatic memory of death, even as he lives. The Incarnation and the crucifixion testify two truths that every mother who has ever lost can understand: God became a baby, and God became a body in which a heart started beating, then stopped. The I AM participated in birth and death *With Us*.

For all the ways our hopes have died, for all the ways the worst has happened, the Paschal mystery extends to us the gift of divine solidarity. Hoping for the best while fearing the worst is some kind of schism for anyone to endure. And it is a schism felt in your deepest self. God is no stranger to this. The body of God keeps vigil with ours, in all its tender, aching places. God does not distance himself from our pain; rather, he puts his skin in our suffering, in a radical act of empathy embodied.

I found consolation in this solidarity, and Holy Saturday gave me a deeper view that year to what great lengths it will go.

The Paschal story holds the death of Good Friday and the silence of Holy Saturday before it breaks into the resurrection joy of Easter Sunday. This is the pattern into which we have been baptized, and there is no telling of the liturgical story that does not include this day of the brutal in-between.

Holy Saturday is the day after the worst has happened—that horrible moment when you wake up, and you remember. Holy Saturday is an unsettling ellipses. It is the wood between the worlds, the eerie silence of a musical rest. It is the brink of living forward into a future in which you fear God is not, as Christ's

followers must have, before the world had any memory of resurrection.

The human heart knows Holy Saturday, because the human
heart knows vigilance—the keeping watch that happens when
the body cannot choose between hope and fear. We know what
it is to wait on edge for the relationship to repair, the addiction
to break, the body to heal, the clarity to come, the kids to get
home safe. We know what it is to *want* in our waiting, and like
the disciples, wonder where God has gone.

Vigilance is holding in tension two dramatically different
outcomes—one of life and one of death—knowing there is nothing you can do to control which way the story tilts. And there is
a place within the liturgical narrative even for this, which we find
at dusk on Holy Saturday, when the Easter Vigil begins.

If the winter solstice is the longest night of the natural year,
Holy Saturday is the longest night of the sacred year. And like
the winter solstice and its Tenebrae of the sky, this night is also
the darkest, and it is in darkness that the vigil liturgy begins.

"This is the night." Worshippers have proclaimed this simple
declaration for centuries, as liturgical scholar Philip Pfatteicher
explains. "It is the night before creation began, the night of exo-
dus from slavery, the night of resurrection all rolled into one event
that is happening here and now."[2] So immersive is this profound
ancient liturgy, that it is as all liturgies are meant to be—not a remembrance of the past, but an embodied participation of a story
happening right now.

Yet it doesn't stay dark for long. At sundown on Holy Saturday, the priest lights a single candle signifying the coming resurrection, and then in a reverse Tenebrae, wick by wick, the light to
the sanctuary is returned.

The Easter Vigil service is comprised of a lengthy, multipart
liturgy that carries through the night until the first light of Easter morning. After the illumination of lights, the worshippers

relive the history of salvation as told through Scripture readings. The vigil then moves traditionally into a service of baptism, as new sons and daughters of God are born through the womb of baptismal waters and spirit. Finally, at the first light of dawn and the resurrection itself, the vigil culminates in the feast of the Easter Eucharist—Jesus is alive, he is known through the breaking of the bread, and the family of God is invited to keep the feast.

Here's what stays with me: The story of God moves through the longest night, but it always ends at a kindred, candlelit table. The story might begin in the void, but it will always end in communion.

The liturgical year's longest night traces the full circle of life with Christ. As Joan Chittister writes, "Here in this single service is the microcosm of the entire Christian life."[3] Because of the resurrection, I believe all things shall be made new. I believe that at the end of the world, there is a table set in love. But I also believe that this side of all-things-new can be hell. Nothing in the Christian story makes this proclamation more plainly than Holy Saturday. And no one has felt this human pain more deeply than Christ himself.

As the Scriptures attest and the Apostles' Creed confirms, "He descended into hell"—there is no darkness into which Jesus has not descended. There is nowhere—not even hell—that Love will not go to bring us back to our deepest belonging.

Morning will break. The alleluias will be returned to us, but make no mistake: The here and now can be a hellscape, strewn over with the shrapnel of broken alleluias. But perhaps this is the strange gift of Holy Saturday: This longest night might become the place where our shattered hopes, how-could-you cries, and spiral-out fears find an honest home. And for all our high vigilance and wounded waiting, we might take heart to know God is with us even in the hellscape.

Holy Saturday does not gloss over nor deny our broken reality, and invites us to name it plainly. It is a day that pronounces our longings and laments belong not only to God, but are holy to God, just as it renounces any claim that these honest expressions are somehow incompatible with the hope that we have. Holy Saturday calls counterfeit on any toxic positivity with which the cross might be vandalized.

I knew now that it was this human God of Holy Saturday who had been with me on the winter solstice, that this is a God who keeps solidarity with us even in the dark.

To question God is no blasphemy. To claim ourselves as beneficiaries of the resurrection, while skipping the tracks of Good Friday and Holy Saturday to get ahead to the "real" one-hit-wonder—now that would be profane. To make ourselves selective witnesses only of new life but not of death, when Jesus incarnated himself fully in both for love—now that would be sacrilege.

The sequence of the story matters: Before the light breaks, before the impossible joy that Jesus lives again, Holy Saturday proclaims that we are seen in our darkest night. Just as Easter proclaims we are never stranded there.

On Easter morning, I woke up expectant, nearing my cycle's end. If I'm honest, I felt God owed me this. Of course the divine promise is presence, never outcome, never circumstance, though I had not yet come to terms with this. My heart was still in the habit of keeping tallies.

I snuck out of bed before Zach got up to see for myself. There was nothing to show, but it was still early yet. We made brown butter pancakes, goat-cheese-topped shakshuka, and topped off our coffee mugs as we settled into the couch for the service. Today, these were our sacraments. It was Zoom church before we ever got used to it. The Easter lilies were virtual, so strange to me then. Still, I put on a bright floral top, which was out of character for my usual black wardrobe; perhaps it was a way for me to dress for joy, even though I didn't feel it yet.

After the service, Zach and I sat out on the porch and took a photo in our Easter quarantine best. I didn't know it then, but it would be the first photo of the three of us.

In the days that followed, I took a test every morning, scrutinizing in every shade of light I could hunt down in the house. But there's nothing that can be done to hasten clarity along. All you can do is wait.

Finally, my secret morning ritual yielded an early morning annunciation. We had buried the alleluias for so long. But now, I would break them forth.

Here we were: a beginning. *Alleluia, alleluia.*

Here I was, praying in plural again. *You are the God who sees us.*

Here we were in Eastertide, and while we had named the night, the call of Easter is to do something arguably more arduous: receive the joy, and this—right after the worst has happened.

Jesus had repeatedly told his disciples that on the third day after his death, he would rise from the dead (Matthew 12:40; 17:22–23; 27:63; Mark 10:34; John 2:19). Yet on the third day, the Gospel of John finds the disciples hidden away behind locked doors, terrified for their lives as they had been known associates of the radical rabbi who had just been executed.

Jesus had told them that joy would be theirs, yet in their fear, they found this too good to be true. Resurrection Day finds them hiding from the greatest news they'd ever encountered.

Brené Brown calls joy the most vulnerable emotion, and for good reason. She writes, "When we lose our tolerance for vulnerability, joy becomes foreboding. No emotion is more frightening than joy, because we believe if we allow ourselves to feel joy, we are inviting disaster. We start dress-rehearsing tragedy in the best moments of our lives in order to stop vulnerability from beating us to the punch."[4]

When joy feels too impossible, too risky to receive, we let fear take over to write the end of the story. When we are unwilling to be surprised by life's goodness, we find ourselves like the disciples: locked away, hiding from life itself, barricading the doors against joy, which we deem as a threat instead of a gift. So we throw down the dead bolt, and live lives that are formed by chronic bracing.

It was incredible how quickly our hopes—once fulfilled—had turned to bracing. Though Zach had known foreboding joy long before we started trying again after loss, so much so that he had written it into his identity. "Getting Smithed," he calls it, the way the fates conspire against his good.

During the opening soccer game of his senior college year, in the final minute of double overtime, Zach made a sliding goal-line save—only to have the ball bounce haphazardly off an on-rushing opponent into the goal after all, while another opponent's kick broke his leg. Everyone who was on the field that day—including me—heard the crack.

When we were dating long distance, he totaled his truck in an accident that was the fault of another driver's just before the trip on which he planned to propose. He had to borrow his brother's car instead, and then *that* car's battery died so we needed a jump (I still said yes).

Zach is the oldest of three boys and they will all sit around at family gatherings trading stories about the time they got scammed, shorted, or otherwise thwarted—the Social Security card lost in the mail, the insurance bill mix-up, the check-engine light coming on only during the private car sale.

It's a family joke and these are just foibles, but for Zach it speaks to something deeper—the founding belief that if it can go wrong, it will go wrong, and for him. Better to just call it now, at least affording yourself the indulgence of being right. This posture feeds into self-fulfilling prophecy, as well as the felt futility of the "Why try?"

Joy was not easy for him. It was not easy for us.

Foreboding joy says: This is too good to believe.

Resurrection says: Believe it. This is a joy you can trust.

It is a tragedy to lose, yes. But it is also a tragedy to spend a life bracing against all given good, dead bolting the door against the bliss that longs to be lived.

Weeks went by slowly and I was continually surprised to find myself still pregnant. Hormones disrupted my sleep and I often woke early, sometimes queasy. I would wake with a dragon stirring in my stomach, and apples sounded divine. I would pluck a Pink Lady from the fridge and give it a quick baptism at the sink, slice it into crescents, and oh this was good. Some gagging when I brushed my teeth. Better after the apple.

My body, this fatigued, apple-craving body, was cocreating with God. Already, cells were composing in secret within me that would live into a future I would not get to touch. It inspired wonder. When Zach put his hand on my stomach, it was as if it were the most precious place in the world.

A story we were prepared to love for a lifetime was just now beginning, particle-small, and we could only hope the storybook would not be slammed shut. Could anything be more vulnerable? It inspired fear.

"The Coronavirus has led the United States to the valley of the shadow of death," wrote Elizabeth Dias in *The New York Times*.

"In just three months, a microscopic particle has laid bare human mortality."[5]

Those first three months mapped onto my first trimester with startling precision, heightening the glare of threat from the outside, as well as the risk within. And so cells began multiplying. Some toward life, or so we hoped, others toward an unprecedented sweep of death.

It was Eastertide now, yet people began calling it "the Longest Lent." It was a collective near-death experience,[6] a chronic confrontation of fight, flight, freeze.

It was Easter, seasonally but also personally—here we were receiving news of life after death. But to me, it felt like a never-ending Holy Saturday. And at the cross-section of my hope and my fear, I found it difficult to breathe.

As we withdrew to the four walls of our home—calendars cleared, trips canceled, presence reduced to tiny grids of faces on a screen—our lives became small, and my anxiety loomed large. It shallowed my breath. I developed a chronic lump in my throat that no swallow could settle. At first I was convinced it was a viral symptom, but it was just fear itself—lodged in my airways.

Constant vigilance holds our bodies in existential toggle: All could be well, or, slanted by just a billionth of a degree's difference, all could be lost. When all you have are the ellipses of unknowing how this story will go, how can any of us breathe easy?

It seemed we were able to get pregnant with relative ease, which I did not take for granted, but the scare was in the hope of *staying* pregnant. It seemed danger was everywhere: toxic aerosols in my hair spray, my night cream, all of which had to be purged in the spirit of precaution. Viral particles swarming unseen at the grocery store for a quick toilet paper pickup. Unfriendly herbal ingredients in my tea, which I scrutinized.

Breath is the divine gift of life, and here I was petrified of other people's exhales. Just as I was petrified that this growing baby inside of me might never take a first breath. To be alive is to be thrust into a labyrinth of risk, and nothing awakened me to this more than a pandemic pregnancy.

The week I conceived, the World Health Organization declared the coronavirus a global pandemic.

As case counts reached fever pitch, new brain cells were multiplying at a hundred a minute.

As restaurants, hair salons, and nonessential businesses shut down, a spine and its nervous system was unfolding like a tender fern head.

As family members hosted funerals on Zoom, and New York City began freezing bodies because there wasn't enough gravesite space, a heart began beating.

How could I reckon with the reality that countless people were losing their lives to a respiratory disease at the same time this baby's lungs were tenderly forming?

I had flinched when the doctor first set my due date: December 22, exactly one year and one day forward from our winter solstice loss.

Everywhere I looked, inside and out, death and life were kindred in ways I never wanted them to be. My mind played the tapes of an almost-death so often, so vividly, that it became a memory though it had never happened.

My doctors assured me this wasn't a high-risk pregnancy, but it is—for all of us—a high-risk life.

Pinning a parent's hope on safe arrival is perfectly valid, and at the same time, I have begun to think it strange that so many of us seem to regard birth as the safe zone, as if it's any safer out of the womb and into the world.

We wait for the yes, the plus sign, the call from the agency, with no way of knowing: *Will this time be the one?* Then we wait for nine months, praying for health and safe passage. Or many more, praying that all the pieces align. And then we wait for the contractions and fight toward the final push, bearing our children into a life that is profoundly sacred in a world that is profoundly unsafe. And there it is, as astonishing as birth itself—the paradox of a lifetime.

Every one of us is born into a world that is subject to deadly viruses, bullying classmates, wildfires and tornado watches, power-hungry despots, melting ice caps. The world where we cry our wholehearted welcomes to newborns is the very world where first-graders don't come home from school and doctors get it wrong and good people fall asleep at the wheel.

This ordinary life is riddled with risk factors and unfavorable odds. We speak of possibility as if it is a beautiful thing, but any moment is ripe with the risk of things slipping south. How can a person live any given Thursday when everything is just the slightest jiggle of the switch away from great good or our undoing?

"Was this parenthood?" author Sinéad Gleeson writes in *Constellations*. "That every second of joy would be atomically split with fear?"[7] Was this life?

I was clutching every contingent future, every what-if, and the weight of it was breaking me. All that breath I was holding, I didn't know how to let it go. Like a question that goes unanswered, I didn't know how to let it land.

After all, what is fear but love biting its lip—bracing, bargaining with God, until blood is drawn.

Some days, my prayers were giant, genuine exhales: *Thank you.* No frills. Other days, I'd wake up and not *feel* pregnant, and too terrified to get out of bed, I'd lie there before the first light praying, "Lord, have mercy. Christ, have mercy."

And then there were days when my prayers became face-offs.

No, I would tell God, as if God is an unruly toddler reaching toward a hot stove. *Not again,* as if it is mine to hold the divine accountable.

Sometimes the force of this surprised even me, yet I wanted to believe my praying in plural was not for naught. I believed God was with us, and I wanted to believe in a future that would hold three of us.

I have always loved the way the church's sacramental life requires us to be up in each other's business. Embodiment and human touch are integral to liturgical practice: baptism, breaking bread, washing of feet, passing the peace, anointing of oil are all acts of physical witness. We encounter God as we encounter each other, and it is meant to be this way. Yet in quarantine, these shared practices were disrupted, including the sacrament of communion, which has always been grounding to me. So without access to the common cup and bread, I created my own grounding practice.

In the hot water stream of my morning shower, I started a new ritual of crossing myself. In the name of the Father, Son, and Holy Spirit, I signed with my hands the truth that I hoped to seal in my heart:

I am beloved.

I belong to the love of God, and nothing else can claim me. The heart that set the story of the world in motion sets the tempo for this life. The breath that breathed spirit into human lungs in the beginning inhales and exhales within me now. This body, this life, is beloved by God; in love, it lives and breathes and has its being.

I am baptized.

This is a baptized body. These waters signify that this body, with all its scars seen and unseen, with all its muscle memory, with all its pleasures and pains and limitations, is united with

Christ and will be raised with Christ. This baptized body is immersed in a story in which love will always have the last word.

Through baptism, we inaugurate the new reality—union with
Christ's life, death, and resurrection—that we will spend the rest
of our lives living and leaning into. "We remember that which is
to come," as Gregory of Nyssa said of the sacrament.[8] In this way,
baptism calls us boldly into hope.

So I crossed myself, if sometimes with shaking hands—the
water a daily echo of an eternal sacrament of my baptismal waters—
as a way of remembering, as a way of saying amen, *May it be so.*

I was two weeks away from my first appointment, when I
would be eight weeks pregnant, when there would be a detect-
able heartbeat or not. And the wait felt just as hard as the one-
week wait I was given at the ER until my appointment to confirm
miscarriage. Remembering who I am became my practice of
hope, and this ritual helped me bring its truth into my body. It
helped me stay with my hope even in this liminal space.

And then came the day when I saw red.

In that moment, my heart left the building, a parachute evacu-
ation, and my reptile brain took over. It assessed: There was no
possible way this would turn out okay. It took action: My rational
self went to Zach at his laptop during our workday and told him
I needed to go in. I did not look at him because I didn't want to
see my greatest fear reflected in his face: that our joy really was
too good to be true; that we'd been bracing for good reason. My
rational self made the call, Zach drove me, but due to Covid re-
strictions, he was not allowed to go in.

I went into the exam room certain that I already knew how
this story would go. But I was wrong. There was a heartbeat and
it belonged to a "perfectly healthy" baby, in my doctor's words. It

was the first time I had heard it, and *seen* this baby, kicking and fully alive on the dark screen. The doctor told me there was a small blood clot, a hematoma, in the uterus, which is not uncommon and should resolve itself soon; but the baby was well and unaffected.

Right away I texted Zach, who was waiting in the parking lot. And I didn't realize how badly my body was clenching, how tightly I was holding my breath, until I released it.

Today there was a heartbeat, and I got to hear it—the meter to the sonnet that would become a life.

Some weeks after that, we would hear the three words "It's a girl!" Now when I prayed in plural, it gave new color and concept to our *we*.

I asked Zach, "Is she going to ruin you? Is she just going to be some little blue-eyed girl you can never say no to?"

"Possibly," he says, eyes twinkling and wisely making no promises.

Soon after that, I would go in for a routine appointment and the Doppler would not be able to find the heartbeat, and I would wait in the exam room for an ultrasound for forty-five minutes. And *I AM, With Us* became the only promise able to steady my inhale and exhale in this suspension of unknowing.

When I came home from this appointment, I showed Zach the new trio of ultrasound images, her profile in spirited swim, and I saw the softness spread on his face like a sunrise. She was a wonder, even the still frames without the motion—the dream-hazed dots of her vertebrae arranged just so, like some stack cairns of river rock. Against all our apprehension, she was starting to feel real to us.

"She's a force and a fury even now," he said, and then: "I'm happy." He had said these words before, and I was surprised at his willingness to voice them again, after what had happened last time. I waited for the qualifier, because he's a Smith, because I know him, but it didn't come. And because he knows me and knew I was waiting, he smiled wryly and added, "Full stop."

And I heard this for what it was: a confession of faith.

He held his hands out to mine, saying, "We should probably start making nursery plans."

It was midsummer now, post-Easter, post-Pentecost. It was supposedly the green season of Ordinary Time, except it was anything but ordinary. In the wake of our painfully invisible loss, and a rapid-rising pandemic, time felt capricious. Before and afters slurred, the calendar's clean gridlines dissolved like ink in water, liminality blooming in its place. I was desperate for a still point amid its churning, a center that might hold, a steadiness that might hold *me*.

More than anything, I needed to find a way to practice hope and steady myself against the spiral of my fear. Joy was here, in the present, because at least for today, I was pregnant. This was a gift that was all grace, but for today, this was joy I wanted to be open to and receive. The morning after the ultrasound scare, I was shaken in the aftershocks of the *almost*. Any hope that I had was now stranded in a neverland of near misses, brushing the wing of the ultimate in too close a call.

I'm so scared, the heart's honest refrain. And for good reason. My fear was valid.

I took deep breaths and went through my morning ritual in the shower to steady myself.

I am beloved, I crossed myself right to left, hot water streaming.

I am baptized, I crossed myself up and down.

Then I put my palm to my chest and added a third confession, *I am badass.*

Because how else might you name the spirit of defiance in daring to remember our baptism even as we remember our death? Because surely it takes a singular kind of courage to practice hope in a high-risk life. Because hope in the *after*, hope against the grain of entirely reasonable fear, in the unknowing of how this story will go, is some kind of badass. And because I want to be the kind of person who stays in the gutsy work of taking heart, of choosing to take on the risks of love.

I'm not impressed by the colloquial swagger of this word as some use it, nor am I offended by it as others might be. Rather, I find we need language to wake us up to the clear-eyed remembrance of who we really are. I never want to forget the audacity of the resurrection that would dare to break every natural law in the universe, just as I never want to forget that the very pulse of this divine life-after-death lives, moves, and breathes within us. I needed (and still need) language to name so rich an inheritance of counterfactual courage.

Whatever your before and afters, whatever your liminal in-between, whatever what-if's might shallow your breath, I believe this much is true:

You are beloved, loved by a God who sings over you and holds you to the heart.

You are baptized, should you choose to be, sustained by a Spirit who anoints you and unites you with the resurrected Christ who is always bringing dead things to life. Or if you're not yet, the waters are always open to you.

And you are a badass, because it takes some kind of courage to hope in a world where God has died. It takes courage to love in a world where nothing is safe. And I'm of the mind that it is good to name what is true. I have to believe it is good to shout the name of our courage into the winds of risk, in the very spirit of resurrection. It is good to wake up to the fight within us, the very fight of life against death that has already been decided.

This I believe: It's a high-risk life, but as Easter tells us plainly, the end of the story is spoken for. The table of joy—the inevitable feast—is set. This is the creed that emboldens us to take heart.

I needed to speak these realities by name because I needed to practice believing they were true of me. I needed to practice believing my belovedness, believing my baptism, believing my badassery. So every morning I began to remember my baptism, cross myself, and say amen, *May it be so.*

The Gospel of John tells it this way: Even though the disciples had locked the doors days after his death, Jesus somehow suddenly shows up among them—fully alive. I love the scene of this—the raw, belly-flipping shock it must have been. Even in their fear, resurrection broke through walls to bring them into joy.

There is nothing holy about making a preemptive strike against joy. There is nothing sacred about deferring delight and goodness where they are to be found. If foreboding joy writes inevitable disaster and death into every good story, Easter tells us the end of the story *has* already been written, and the end is life. We feast at Easter, the central Christian celebration, as preview of this final feast that calls us to practice it even now as we wait for a world to be made whole.

The call is not to disqualify, hedge, or hesitate. The call of Easter—and every Sunday that the sacred year considers a "little Easter"—is to *keep* the feast. And the feast is kept by taking notice and celebrating wherever God is found doing a new thing, wherever the Spirit is breathing new life, wherever joy is breaking through the walls of our fear, as we anticipate the final feast in which our future is sealed.

While Holy Saturday affirms the realness of human pain and

waiting, Easter invites us to allow ourselves to be astonished by resurrection, even in a Holy Saturday world. Joy, like resurrection, requires a certain willingness to be surprised, confounded even. It asks us to say yes to bewilderment. Yet when we release our tightfisted foregone conclusions, our hands can open to receive new gifts that break through and beyond the grid of our expectations.

After the worst has happened, even though we have every reason to fear a foreboding future, resurrection gently calls us to rewild our joy. When we can soften into its gifts, we might find we become people shaped by hope and joy, rather than people formed in the bracing. We might find ourselves beautifully bewildered.

7

STAYING WITH YOUR BREATH

Ordinary Time

I AM fire and spirit
With You in all the places that call upon your
*   strength*

Pain is a formidable force. But so am I.

DIANA SPALDING, Jill Koziol, and Liz Tenety,
The Motherly Guide to Becoming Mama

Life can't always be high holidays and high-octave key changes, and the liturgical year makes no ask of us to live at perpetual peak. Instead, it gives us Ordinary Time—the longest season in the sacred year, in which, at first glance, it would appear not much happens. If you were to look at the liturgical calendar as it is often visualized as a wheel, most of the wheel is green—the liturgical color for this season of "ordinal" or simply counted days. Stretching from the day after Pentecost through the lush summer months and first of fall until the first Sunday of Advent, Ordinary Time is often the in medias res of life—the story in the middle—and this would be easy to pass by, except the green season is where the growth happens.

The liturgical year tells two stories as they converge: the life of Christ as he enters human time, and the life of the church, as we enter God time. The green season commences after the major events of the resurrection and Pentecost and is our invitation to keep time with God by bringing this sustaining life force and fire into our daily lives, rather than allowing them to remain unlived, stranded in abstraction.

These are the days of hitting snooze, remembering trash day, and reheating Tuesday's leftovers. And these are the days in which God's people are called to live out the power of Christ's resurrection in our real time. Because even though our story is still unfolding in the here and now, the final word has already been written, and we practice it by faith.

The green season is the proving ground for all we profess to believe during the high seasons.

And it should tell us something that Ordinary Time is the longest liturgical season, because resurrection needs a lot of practice, the practice of a lifetime.

For us that year, our Ordinary Time began with big news— Zach was offered a teaching position based in the mid-Atlantic where we both grew up, and we decided to move forward. So that summer, we made the trek from Tennessee and its Smoky Mountains back up north to Pennsylvania's capital city, and moved into an old brick rowhouse blocks away from the Susquehanna riverfront. For the first time in a decade, we would be just an hour or two's drive from the places we grew up, and from our families. It was for us a season of settling in—we made our new house a home, painted a nursery, and prepared for a family of three. Meanwhile, the moon of my body was waxing from crescent to full.

What could be more ordinary than the breath? Breathing is so synonymous with life itself that it might be considered "the most human thing we all do," as author and psychologist Hillary

McBride writes. The inhale is "the first thing that babies do earth-side, and exhale is the last thing that bodies do before death."[1]

We breathe on average twenty thousand breaths every day. Breathing is so reflexive that it is rare that we give any breaths conscious thought. And yet, the ordinary breath becomes nothing less than sacramental when we recognize that with each inhale and exhale, we speak the name of God.

In *Dancing in God's Earthquake,* Rabbi Arthur Waskow describes the transformative moment of his realization that the name God reveals of Godself in the Old Testament—*YHWH* in Hebrew—is "unpronounceable because 'YHWH,' with no vowels, is just a Breath."[2] "The notion of YHWH as 'the Breath of Life' accords with a deep sense of God as intimate and transcendent at once," he writes. "If we have no breath in us, we die."[3]

Some speak of God as being closer than our breath, and I have always liked this juxtaposition: something as ordinary as the breath in constant communion with something as ultimate as the presence of God.

The breath grounds us in the present, the here and now, which is where God meets us. And the breath of God—the Spirit—ushers us into sacred time through the liturgical year where Christ meets us in every human moment. Staying with our breath, we stay with our life. And staying with the story of the liturgical year becomes the profound practice of staying with the life of Christ, which always leads into resurrection.

It makes me wonder: What might our lives look like if we turned to our inhale and exhale as a spiritual practice? As a way of returning to our life source, our essential belovedness?

What if—within Ordinary Time—we turned to the ordinary breath as a way of practicing presence to the God who is ever-present with us?

"Listen," writes Mary Oliver, "are you breathing just a little, and calling it a life?"[4]

The sad truth is that most of us are.

Every one of us is born knowing exactly how to take a deep, diaphragmatic breath. Even though we've never experienced oxygen in our lungs in our water world of before, breathing is the instant intuition of us all from moment one.

It's this deep inhale of a new world and its strange air that powers the exciting part for parents: the inaugural sound-off of that which will belong to them for a lifetime—the first cry. One's very voice. This is how we come into the world: breathing deeply to settle ourselves when reality comes crashing like a shock of cold water. To live is to breathe, and babies are born knowing how. We are born proficient in this vital power. You might say the diaphragmatic breath is our birthright.

Yet how quickly we unlearn this essential skill. How quickly stress descends, quickens and shallows our inhale. Our first language is the full-throated bellow, yet soon we are initiated into the school of restraint. Especially for anyone whose voice and presence are easily dismissed by their surrounding majority culture. Especially for women, who are taught from a young age to play by the rules, blend into the background, and never take up too much space, literally and figuratively. We are conditioned not to get too loud or too ambitious, and that our value increases with physical smallness, so we develop certain reflexes: apologizing for our voice and presence, sucking in our stomachs as second nature.

Over time and its slow erosion by stress and social conditioning, we lose touch with the breath, the diaphragm, the core in which this first instinct lives. We become slowly estranged from the muscles that are designed to steady and support us through any crisis, come what may. I know I had.

Until I am a woman months away from her due date, bracing for unprecedented pain, fighting to stay afloat, alive, not dead in a pandemic in which circulating air itself is cause for panic. Until I am a woman standing belly out on a yoga mat, trying to remember what she was born knowing how to do.

A lifetime of fighting, flying, freezing is embedded in my muscle memory, and that is what I am facing off in my wobbly warrior pose as I practice taking one deep breath, and then another.

How strange, I think, to be fighting so hard to learn something that will be effortless for my daughter from moment one. Even now, she is my teacher.

As an adult I made peace with my body as much as anyone can, but I was not in touch with my strength. I was an intermittent exerciser, an every-now-and-then practitioner, but movement was not part of my daily, weekly rhythms.

But once we went public with news of our pregnancy, the labor part started to feel more real, more impending, and more terrifying than ever.

My fear was multifaceted.

On a physical level, I am not a high-pain-tolerance person. I loved learning about what was happening inside of me—the baby's weekly progression from apricot to lemon to avocado. It was the coming-out-of-me part that I painstakingly avoided. My pregnancy books were underlined and earmarked, except for the final chapters, where the show got real. Which detailed what would happen to *me* when fruit metaphors would give violent way to other metaphors: pain like a freight train, like a riptide— pulling you under, slamming you into the sand.

On a psychological level, my anxieties surrounding this intense event in my near future were intensified by the present pandemic and memory of miscarriage. I knew by now there was nothing safe about birth, for me or for her. No outcome was secure.

This pregnancy had begun just as the global pandemic was declared, and our daughter's due date would be coinciding with what epidemiologists were already calling America's deadliest winter in modern memory. I was afraid I would end up laboring alone, as some hospitals weren't allowing partners in the delivery room. I was afraid of being in the same building, sharing the same air duct system, as the Covid floor, after months of meticulous caution.

Finally, I was going to have to get serious about training. "We are too often treated like babies for having babies when we should be in training," Louise Erdrich writes in *The Blue Jay's Dance*, "like acolytes, novices to the high priestesshood, like serious applicants for the space program."[5]

The average woman in labor, I learned, expels not just as much air as a runner during a marathon but *three times as much.*[6] I couldn't fathom ever voluntarily signing up for a marathon, let alone showing up to a marathon without any training, showing up to a gravity-less galaxy without the rigors of mental, emotional, physical preparation.

I didn't know what to expect, but I knew labor was going to call upon muscles I never even knew I had, and I wanted to be well acquainted with them long before I needed them most. I wanted desperately to go into labor trusting my body, which meant that now was my time to practice my strength.

Where—like many women—I had silenced my body, I would have to learn to listen.

Where I had sought control, I would need to learn to surrender.

Where I had regarded with suspicion, I would need to learn to trust.

After all, an entire original person my body had grown from scratch was about to exit my body through unprecedented pain, and the coping mechanism they were giving me was *breathing* and a couple of ice chips? Or, of course, a needle, though I was also terrified of those.

We were going to have to take our relationship to the next level, my body and I. And like any relationship, I was going to have to put the time in.

A woman on the screen introduced herself as three months postpartum, with another woman who was twenty weeks pregnant with twins, and another who was thirty-six weeks along. Together, they stood before an exposed brick wall in leggings and sports bras in calming hues of clay and lavender. I was four months away from my due date, and for the first time I now had a working Google Doc titled "Birth Plan" and a subscription to a streaming birth prep workout program recommended by ob-gyns and physical therapists.

Today was the first day of my program, and today all they wanted from me was to breathe, which felt like something I could do.

"The way that you breathe is vital to your core and pelvic health," the instructor named Brooke said while she balanced on a yoga ball, and guided me to put my hands on my rib cage and feel its expansion as I took a deep inhale.

Of all the word pictures used to describe women's reproductive health, I liked the ones that imbue dignity, beauty, the sacred, even. The pelvic floor is commonly described as a hammock, but Brooke used a description I haven't heard before. "Think about your pelvic floor as a diamond," she said. "A diamond that expands as you inhale, and returns to neutral as you exhale."

I'd been learning quite a bit about pelvic health. The pelvic floor is a group of muscles designed to support the uterus, bladder, and bowels, and as the base of one's core, contributes to overall bodily stability. These muscles uniquely support a woman in pregnancy, pushing through labor, and postpartum recovery, though pelvic health is linked to overall health for all women, and men, as well. Symptoms of a weakened pelvic floor often feel intensely personal, painful, and stigmatized as they are rarely talked about even if commonly experienced, such as loss of bladder and bowel control (incontinence), pain during sex, ab separation (diastasis recti), or prolapse (the dropping of the uterus, rectum, or bladder from their usual position).

But pelvic floor therapists unanimously agree: It doesn't have to be this way. No one needs to simply put up with these highly treatable issues. And that's why I was here, hands on my rib cage—to both prepare my body for birth and do what I could to prevent such intimate injuries from happening in the first place.

From her lavender yoga ball, Brooke spoke. Through this program, she explained, "You will learn to locate your pelvic muscles and to activate them. You will learn to repattern your breath to serve you and support you, in labor, in birth, and in your everyday life."

All of this was practice, I was told, for when the real contractions come calling, and the core's strength is needed most. "The breath," Brooke said, "is how we get these muscles to talk to each other, to work together."

For every contraction that shouts to the body *run, run, run!* the breath voices its bold counter: *all is well, all is well, all is well.* In the midst of profound emotional or physical pain, the diaphragmatic breath is able to lift us out of the autonomic nervous system's stress response and bring us back to our "rest and digest" state, also known as the parasympathetic nervous system. The deep breath slows the heartbeat, lowers blood pressure, and stabilizes the nervous system, ushering a person from high-alert adrenaline back to baseline calm.

"Between stimulus and response there is a space," psychologist and author Viktor Frankl once said. "In that space is our power to choose our response. In our response lies our growth and our freedom."[7] As I rolled out my yoga mat every night after dinner, I began to think of this space as diamond shaped. A diamond within that presents all of us with a choice, when faced with the stimulus of any threat, physical or psychological.

Here, a space where we can hold our stress, freezing, clenching, straining. Or, a place where we can hold space for our expanding power. Here, a place to practice the ordinary breath of Ordinary Time, an invitation to get our inner muscles to talk to each other, so when the crisis comes, we're ready.

Over the coming weeks, I would learn something called the "S" breath, a tool for novices like me to locate the pelvic floor muscles and activate them with the full core. This exercise might be thought of as a supercharged Kegel, which is classically prescribed for women's sexual health and labor prep. Yet while the Kegel only fires the floor of the core's cylinder, the "S" breath trains to fire the core as a full unit. First, you take a deep inhale, then on the exhale, let out an audible "Ssssss," which will naturally draw your pelvic floor upward and your abdominals inward toward your belly button, in a full 360-degree core activation around the torso. This was much of the program—engaging the core muscles on the exhale, and bringing awareness to this pattern through every exercise set and repetition.

And so a muscle builds, breath by breath.

I would learn all about these muscles, whose intricate workings were formerly unknown to me.

Your diaphragm is a muscle at the base of your lungs, the top of your core. Your pelvic floor is a concave set of muscles that support from below. Your spine supports from the back, and abdominals from the front. Together, these muscles create a cylinder-shaped space through which oxygen flows in rhythms of inhale and exhale, tension and release. This pressure chamber is known as your core.

The core has been characterized as a tin can, something you toss into the recyclables. But I began to think of it as a cathedral dome, a sanctuary at the center of the self where our greatest strength is sourced. Because this is what I was just beginning to understand. Here, within the core, we find our fortitude to withstand any force that might trigger our fight, flight, or freeze response. Here, we find the ability to release the stress of any threat, and return to the breath that sustains our life and well-being.

Consider it: Just by breathing, we can come home to ourselves. If the body is a temple, surely the core is its holy of holies. The place where nothing less than the spirit of God—the origin of life—stirs our every breath. The place where the most elemental liturgy of our lives happens: inhale, exhale, inhale, exhale.

What could be more ordinary than the rhythm of the breath? And yet the humble inhale and exhale is the exchange upon which we shape our lives.

The here and now is where any pain we feel is most acute. Yet this place, this time, are the exact coordinates of sacred encounter. The trouble comes when we believe we are alone—unseen, unaccompanied—in life's many contractions. But we are not left to our own devices after all. God meets us in the very place in which we find ourselves: the present moment in which our blood is pumping and our lungs are expanding and our nervous system is firing. The love that is ancient-present, ever new, rises to meet us in our now.

Jewish mystic and philosopher Martin Buber writes, "All real living is meeting."[8] And this encounter happens at our core: the breath of God, which is spirit, in intimate exchange with the breath of our life. The *I AM With Us*—the being of God in communion with our being at the very center of the self.

Life is full of contractions, that which stretches us to our limits, twists and turns us inside out. And peace speaks its name to us in a breath: *I AM, I AM, I AM. With You, With You, With You.*

I was learning so much. And as I did, fascination of the body began crowding out some of my fear of labor. Prior to my birth prep, I had a vague notion of what the core is, but I mostly thought it was about abs, and ab work was never going to be my thing. I could not have drawn you a diagram. I could not have told you any of the benefits of "core health," or how the breath was remotely related to these essential muscles.

So, then. What I was realizing was that true core strength was not about bodybuilding, but about breathing. Which means anyone can do it, because everyone does.

"This is your contraction!" Brooke would say as we held deep squats, my thighs aflame and shaking with exertion. And every time I felt the burning pull to cave, she would cut me off at the very thought: "Stay with it! You won't be able to pull out of your contractions, so don't pull out now!" It was maddeningly rational, her pitch: "All you have to do is stay with your breath, for three . . . two . . . aaaaand one."

I can't pinpoint the exact moment it happened. Rather, somewhere along the line of a thousand deep core holds, pelvic tilts, and bear crawls, when the muscle fatigue gave way to something that felt like strength, a knowing began to rise within me. *Wait*, I thought. *Wait*. So what you're telling me is the greatest defense a person can have against the stress response is something as simple as the breath? You're telling me that I have had access to this stabilizing power my whole life, and for most of that life, I have been asleep to it?

Have we really been holding our breath for a lifetime?

Not everyone will have the physical experience of giving birth, of course. Neither would I presume to claim that labor has the corner on the ultimate pain, the human spectrum of which is unfortunately vast and varied. But all of us have a lifetime's worth of stress response experiences, when the body is thrust into fight, flight, or freeze.

This is your contraction.

Life is full of them. We will all experience threats to our physical, emotional, mental, spiritual well-being. We will all face disproportionate pressures beyond what we imagine we can bear that send us into a desperate search for every available resource we have to stay standing. We all have our reasons for holding our breath.

All you have to do is stay with the breath.

And all of us harbor a cathedral within that is capable of bringing us back to center. In the literal and biological sense, the core is the center of the body, and breathing is the vital process that happens at the center of our core. If it is stability we seek, we will find it here.

Perhaps the breath is not so ordinary after all. When life takes us to our limit, our greatest resource of resilience has been with us all along. In any crisis, we can stay grounded by staying with our breath, and we can summon our deepest strength by activating our core. Through the core-activated breath, you are strengthening the exact same muscle sets that are capable of bringing a new human being into the world. Through the breath, you are returning to your birthright, your intuition from moment one.

Just as a woman in labor is called to stay with her breath to bring forth new life, the liturgical year calls us to stay with the story that leads into new life.

This kind of hope is not wispy, wishful thinking; it is a dead lift from one's core. It takes a certain strength to keep your hopes up, to engage the muscles of your core, and lift, lift, lift—against the entropy of everything, against the gravity of death itself. To keep such a hope up is to set the total weight of your being against "the full catastrophe of living,"[9] and in doing so, grit your teeth, fire every muscle you have, and feel the burn of the sweat-beaded *push*.

The way of mortal time is entropy—to lie low. Yet the way of love is to lift up, and this requires a full recruitment of our deepest muscles—"where the spirit meets the bone."[10] And yet this is no bootstrap endeavor. We are not tasked to do any of this in our own strength, but in the borrowed strength of Christ's resurrection power. When we stand our ground in so great a counter-story, as pastor and author Osheta Moore so memorably puts it, we find our foundations to push from a place of borrowed power—as outsized strength meets outsized strength.[11]

This is what it means to activate our core, when we understand it not as a burden beyond our abilities, but as a call to lean into the nerve of God and find the support we need when we need it most. We go into this inner cathedral with courage, knowing that God meets us there, taking heart that the very counter rhythms of resurrection animate our every push. This is the gutsy work, and we do not do it alone.

The breath that spoke life into the first human lungs, that stirred Pentecost wind and fire, that breathes spirit into dry bones is the strength that is with us now. The voice of God rings out over the valley of dry bones rattling back to life: "I will put my spirit within you, and you shall live, and I will place you on your own soil" (Ezekiel 37:14). This is the way of breath: to bring life, to settle, to anchor, to bring home.

And this strange, gorgeous grace is alive in us in our here and now, and it is ever leading us into resurrection.

Can you imagine bringing that kind of power into your day-to-day life, in the humble cycle of Ordinary Time? Can you imagine giving yourself the shores of such astonishing support? The support has always been there. The question is: Are we awake to it?

I once heard the story of a woman standing on the white sand coastlines of Florida. She was in her fifties. She had never seen the ocean until just then.

Her name is Dorris. "I was trapped in a ten-block radius for well over twenty years," she says. Her life moved through the same loops of violence, the same cycle of in and out of jail before getting back out onto the streets. The same contractions over and over, yet they never led to the life she hoped for. She sold her body as the only thing she had to sell, and for twenty-six years, tried to numb the pain of her past with drugs that, in her words, did not love her back. On the streets of Nashville where she lived, she reckoned with the possibility that she might die every single day. Even still, she walked the streets reciting psalms from her childhood, praying for God to come and get her out.

Her mother was praying, too, after many years of not knowing when she might get the call that her daughter was gone. Through the invitation of a friend, Dorris was invited to enter the program at Thistle Farms, a social nonprofit that provides housing, healthcare, therapy, and employment to women survivors of addiction and trafficking. With the core belief that "Love heals every body," Thistle Farms produces candles, soaps, and other body products, creating a pathway to financial freedom for its employees.

Dorris graduated from the two-year program and "got [her] life back."[12] Then she came on staff as a speaker and organizer and ultimately events director, telling her story and the story of love's transformation across the country to Thistle Farms's national network of sister organizations.

I once heard Becca Stevens, the founder of Thistle Farms and an Episcopal priest, tell the story of when Dorris's work took her to Florida, where she saw the ocean for the first time. She kicked off her shoes with the rest of the team and walked the beach, water rushing up to greet their toes. Becca remembers Dorris was uncharacteristically quiet as she walked the sand. You could hear the tide breathing upon the shore. The view was all sea and sky, so much blue on blue. So far away from that square mile of asphalt and alleyways where she once thought she would live out the rest of her days.

"God did a good job," Dorris said, nodding. Then she threw back her head and flung her arms wide, inquiring to the open shore: "Has it been doing this my whole life?"

Yes, breathes the Spirit. *Yes!* The I AM has always been With You. God has been moving in rhythms of resurrection our whole lives, his love as present and steady to us as the waves that breathe upon the shore.

"He chased me until I found him," Dorris says. "I finally turned around."

The sea has always been there. The spirit of resurrection has always been bringing dead things to life. Sometimes we just have to turn around.

"Something interesting about the nervous system is that the body won't release tension until it feels support," one of my program instructors told us.

And the breath, firing from the pelvic floor throughout the core, is perhaps the greatest psychosomatic support we have. The power of the breath is ours to bear life—for some, a new life, but for all of us, our own.

With every breath, the diaphragm, the pelvic floor, the abdominal muscles move as one, strengthening our deep core. With every breath, we receive the fresh energy of vitalizing oxygen, and release expended, stale energy we no longer need.

Finding your voice, standing your ground, leaning in—metaphors for self-advocacy abound for women today. These mantras are all crafted as counters to the social conditioning of women to be silent, compliant, make ourselves small. And none of these are possible without the pelvic floor, perhaps the most direct metaphor for self-support that we have.

The pelvic floor is the base of our very being in a precarious world. This diamond-shaped space is the foundation of our bodies, and it sets the tone for how we carry ourselves, determining the difference between living stuck in a state of emergency as suspended in the fight-flight-freeze response or living from a state of core-powered stability, as centered by the deep breath.

As such, it is both tragedy and bitter comedy that the muscles that most greatly contribute to our daily well-being are often the most overlooked. If body fluency is about listening to the language of our physical lives, pelvic health is the glaring omission from our embodied education. I couldn't believe that I had made it into my thirties, that it took something as life-altering as a pregnancy, for me to wake up to this vital system that has always been at work in my body. I thought of the pelvis only vaguely as a body part, a flat anatomy factoid.

No one had ever told me it was a power I could flex. But now that I knew, I couldn't imagine living a single day *without* bringing its powers of stability into everything I do.

Imagine what life might look like if we returned our attentions to this inherent system of support. What if, instead of reserving our deep core muscles for a "special occasion" crisis, we brought their strength into our everyday lives through every inhale and exhale? What if we committed ourselves to the diaphragmatic breath: with every inhale, drawing from the depth of reserves available to us; with every exhale, freely releasing the stress that would otherwise keep us stuck in its hold?

What if we released any learned tendency to "suck in" and make ourselves small, which is one of the surest ways to weaken the core?

What might life look like if we lived in communion with the cathedral of our core—this sacred space where God breathes life into our lungs?

What might our lives look like if we lived them within this steady tempo of self- and divine support?

Instead of breathing from the shallows, what if we returned our inhale to its deepest reserves? Instead of making ourselves small through constricting our stomachs and sucking in, what if we actively consented to our expansion? Instead of holding our tension taut within our bodies, what if we rediscovered the core as the home and holding place of our greatest power?

A diamond, a cathedral, a hammock, a cereal bowl: You can pick your own metaphor. But the greater reality it represents is the same: Our pelvic floor, as the foundation of our core, is a space where we source our deepest stability and strength. It's where we hold space for ourselves: our wholeness, our well-being, our greatest defense against whatever stress response life sends our way. Every inhale and exhale is bringing us home to ourselves and the strength we need most.

Shauna Niequist writes of a friend who was in a session with his spiritual director. He was chronicling the great disappointments of his life when, "all at once the usually reserved priest broke in and yelled his name. 'These are the terms! Now what's the invitation?'"[13]

These are the terms: Every one of us is loosed into a world where anything can happen, nothing is secure, and anxiety has a hell of an imagination. We are haunted by whole kingdoms of hypotheticals—ghost futures spiraling out in every direction. And when the contractions come calling and the what-ifs start wilding, our vital systems begin to clench.

It's enough to make anyone forget how to breathe.

I read that newborns learn to breathe from their mothers, by syncing the rhythms of their heart rate, their inhale and exhale, to hers. In the closeness of chest to chest, they learn the most vital sign. Heart to heart, they learn how to *live*.

So maybe that's the invitation: Stay close to the beating heart of love, stay with your breath by pairing and pacing it to the divine breath of the love that holds you. The love that, like the sea, has always been there. Listen to the steadiness of its pulse toward you: *I AM, With Us,* in unchanging rhythm. Let love be the tempo, trust its steadiness, lean in close.

Deep into my second trimester, as the calendar tilted from Ordinary Time toward Advent, I was doing yoga with my sister Rebecca when she started laughing at my "S" breath.

"What are you doing?" she asked me, popping up from her mat. I was laughing then, too, falling out of my downward dog, because it was so second nature to me by then that I forgot how it might sound to others. I tried to explain the technique to her, telling her about the core activation on the exhale.

"It's like the exhale powers your whole body," I said.

"And that's what happens during labor, I guess? That's the breathing pattern people are always talking about?"

"It helps," I said. "Or at least, it's supposed to. Never done it before—will report back!"

She rose up on her mat and put her palms together as if in prayer, giving me a deep namaste bow. "May the pelvic force be with you."

I bowed back. "And also with you." We laughed at this new kind of call and response. But it was, a month before my daughter's arrival, a very serious prayer of mine. Maybe it is for all of us.

8

PRACTICING INCARNATION

Advent, Again

I AM the Word made flesh
With You in every labor of life

> We are all meant to be mothers of God. For God is always needing to be born.
>
> MEISTER ECKHART

Several years ago, Zach and I were at a Lessons and Carols service at the downtown cathedral when the music was overtaken by sirens from the street, red lights reeling through the window arches. I have thought about Advent like this ever since: ambulance lights refracted through stained glass. Hallelujahs of the midnight clear met with the minor keys of distress signals. This is the world into which Love comes, and Advent is our time to sing as sirens, casting out our hope like emergency flares into the dark and silent night: "Come, Lord Jesus, Come . . ."

"Advent always begins in the dark," Fleming Rutledge writes.[1] It begins in bold-faced recognition of the way things are but should not be. And there was so much that should not be. This Advent was punctuated by the sirens of a sweeping pandemic then at its peak, political chaos, systemic injustice and police brutality that takes the lives of those God loves. Advent will always come into a world where power is abused, human rights are denied, and death comes too soon.

Advent expresses the ache of a world waiting to be made right, the waiting between two arrivals: the arrival of the Christ child's birth, and the return of the resurrected Christ to make all things new.

"Advent calls for a life lived on the edge," Rutledge writes. "It can well be called the Time Between. . . . The disappointment, brokenness, suffering, and pain that characterized life in this present world is held in dynamic tension with the promise of future glory that is yet to come. In that Advent tension, the church lives its life."[2]

Living in the tension will always stretch us. And yet in the Incarnation, hope is given what we are all given: a body, and a life to be lived.

As the days crossed into December, I found myself living on a strange continuum: every day carried me further from that final winter solstice night in which I shared a body with our first, and every day carried me closer to our daughter's due date. One year ago, my body had gone into labor for the first time. Now I waited for contractions to again come calling to tell what I hoped would be a very different kind of birth story. It certainly felt like a Time Between. This circle of a year, December to December, Advent to Advent, held so much.

What was a woman to make of this except to feel it all: ache and anticipation, sear of loss and fire of love. I stretched taut in all directions. If love is such expansion, then let me expand. Let my love grow eschatological: reaching forward, reeling back. Let it rake the sky and shake the boughs of the stars until the future is now and the long ago is vibrantly here.

There is a future, however far, in which we will be together again—when the brittle borders of mortal time finally break. For now, I wanted to be reminded of the ways we are interconnected.

In pregnancy, a small measure of fetal cells make a mysterious migration—crossing the placenta to home in their mother's bloodstream, breast tissue, brain, and other organs, even grafting into her heart tissue. A woman in her third trimester of pregnancy might have up to 6 percent of fetal DNA circulating in her bloodstream.[3] Studies support the leading theory that this comingling of cells happens with every pregnancy, even those that end in miscarriage. Scientists call it microchimerism, named for the chimera of Greek mythology, a creature composed of many creatures—lion, goat, and dragon.

This concentration of fetal cells naturally wanes after pregnancy, yet their presence remains in the mother's body for decades, even a lifetime. The oldest woman in one study, for instance, was ninety-four years old, and yet her body still harbored the Y chromosomes of her decades-ago-born son.[4]

Is free-floating DNA enough for those who long to live life together? Hardly. No. But if anything is true, it must be true not only in large scale, but at the smallest. And it seems to me that our bodies tell the story of the great belonging for which we are meant, and this belonging runs deep—down to the veins, down to a single twist of double helix.

It was Advent again, and I wondered what it might mean to have sister cells swimming together in my bloodstream for a lifetime. What it means to be carried in the circulation of our mothers through the turning of the years. What it means to carry our children, long after they have left our bodies—for something other to become part of you, to remain.

If the pattern of any double helix is a signature unto its own, unlike any other, then the body of a mother speaks such a name for life. Kept close—closer than just about anything—in the sanctuary of her pulse.

Surely we are creatures meant to be kindred and carried—by our mothers, by each other, by God.

"The origins of Advent are the body of a woman," says author and liturgist Cole Arthur Riley. "We're talking about a story where God embodies in such vulnerability to entrust Godself to the womb of a human woman."[5] Riley speaks of the sacred darkness of the womb—a place of gestation, beginnings.

In the final weeks and days leading up to my due date, I considered the womb—at its most basic definition—as a muscle. And not just any muscle.

We know muscle, the ribbed force of tissue fibers whose design it is to contract and relax. Through these rhythms, our strength is practiced. What is less known, and rarely acknowledged, is that the uterus is the most powerful muscle in the human body, and it belongs uniquely to women. For all the brute force claims and caricatures of masculinity, this is an undisputed biological fact. The uterus exerts more pressure than any other muscle—it is the only one that possesses the power capable of bringing a new human into the world.

And its power is an unsung wonder.

Prior to pregnancy, the uterus is approximately the size of a closed fist. Over the course of pregnancy, this circular organ expands and expands and expands to achieve what no other muscle can claim: stretching its capacity to five hundred to a thousand times its prepregnancy size.[6] At the time of birth, the uterus weighs approximately two pounds, yet its strength reaches mysteriously beyond itself to push out a baby three to five times its own weight.

What other soft tissue asks so much of us? What other muscle so dramatically alters the borders of the self? The ask is exponential. And yet it is outrageously commonplace: The only reason any of us got here is because a woman braved her yes to so radical an ask.

"When we give birth, we do so from our core," I underlined in my pregnancy book. "Not just the core of our bodies, but the core of ourselves."[7]

Every muscle gains its strength by pushing back against the natural law of gravity. But none so much as this muscle of women, which pushes back against the entropy of all things to proclaim, in the resonant words commonly attributed to Maya Angelou, "Here comes life."

Where entropy declares our destiny is to be laid low, labor is a fight through water, blood, breath, and spirit to say otherwise. For all of death's gravitational pull down to dust, every muscle-powered contraction pushes back in counterargument: *Today, a story begins.*

In the beginning of all beginnings, God is a woman swaying her hips with hope, a woman who says, "Let us stretch. Let us risk. Let us make room."

She stretched and she stretched until her capacity was wide as the night, holding every human soul in the spaciousness of her belonging. And so the circle of the Trinity expands. God is not just with-child, but with-cosmos. Her heart quickens when she thinks of them one by one: *Beloved, Beloved, Beloved.*

In Advent, we hear the ancient echoes of this genesis: *Here comes life.*

Scholar and theologian Phyllis Trible writes in her trailblazing study that the Hebrew words for "womb" and "mercy" share the same root, are kindred at an etymological level. "In its singular form the noun *rebem* means 'womb' or 'uterus,'" she writes. "In the plural, *rabamim,* this concrete meaning expands to the abstractions of compassion, mercy, and love."[8]

Like the widening circles of a stone skipped across a lake, like a muscle that stretches its capacity a thousand times over, mercy is known by its expansiveness. By its encompassing inclusivity, the sweep of every human care in the history of time under a gentle wing.

Trible calls it God's "womb-love," mercy, a circle where God has always held space for us. "The womb protects and nourishes but does not possess and control. It yields its treasure in order that wellness and whole-being might happen. Truly, it is the way of compassion."[9]

Truly, the most powerful muscle in the world.

This "womb-love" of God can be traced in a continuous thread from the Old Testament into the New Testament, where we find Jesus using birth language as a primary paradigm for salvation. To enter the Kingdom, Jesus tells the inquiring Nicodemus, one must be "born again" (John 3:3–8). It's a vivid image: God as one who carries, labors, and gives birth.

If Advent begins with the body of a woman, we are wise to consider what its incarnation asks of our bodies, our lives. This story tells of God making radical room for creation, and Mary making radical room for God—surely this is the way of love, and love now calls to us.

Far from what the surface sentimentality of the season would suggest, to let love be formed within you is inevitably an intimate transformation. It does not merely touch you, as if a gentle hand brushes one's back, it alters your very composition—a change of deep tissue, interior nerve. To let love be formed within you is the bold consent to change shape, to undergo a transformation that is nothing less than the rearrangement of vital organs, of inner life as much as embodied self. Such transformation is the very work of incarnation.

In the stable's dark of that night long ago, Mary's body becomes the first table. Long before Jesus said, "This is my body, broken for you," Mary's body broke for him. Long before the first baptism, it was Mary's water that broke. The cup of her womb, having been so blessed and lifted up, is now poured out. It is the salt of her sweat and blood upon the hay. It is her offering, "Take and eat," to a newborn God, who will one day make this very offering to the world. She is the one who showed him how. And we are the ones still receiving this gift.

The first Eucharist is sacrament given by none other than a woman.

"Heaven cannot hold him," we sing in the Christmas carol "In the Bleak Midwinter," but Mary's muscle will. And we hear the echo of her exponential yes in all of us, in all the places where we stretch to make room for love.

The New York Times weekend review began, "This was one of the most devastating weeks in the U.S. since the coronavirus pandemic began nine months ago."[10] What a nine months it had been. And now my due date would require me to be at the hospital at the very peak of the virus in our city, while there was not yet a vaccine in sight.

The hospital allowed only one support person, so Zach would be with me and had prepared to be my birth partner, but I would not have the assistance of a doula, which I had hoped for.

I cringe, I cry, I recant to think of the myths I once believed about pregnancy, about birth—what it makes of a baby, of a woman. Nothing basic about it. This is the stuff of legend.

Still, legend or not, labor was coming for me soon and it would be bringing pain.

So I came up with an idea, and reached out to a small group of friends for their help.

In an email, I confided some of my concerns about my upcoming due date:

> I don't know how I will react to my body's memory of miscarriage when I go into labor, and don't want the physical sensations to trigger emotional associations of a very different setting.
>
> And to state the obvious, I've never done this before! We'll go in with our best-laid plans, and also know we'll need to be open to the unexpected.
>
> For these unknowns, I'd be grateful for your prayers. And I'd also love your help building my playlist as one of my coping strategies. Actually I have two: one in the genre of "calm focus" and another I'm calling "fight songs." Would you be willing to send me a nomination (or as many as you'd like!) for these playlists?
>
> I imagine being surrounded by these gifts of yours during this intense time will renew my courage when I need it most. Thank you so much for any tracks you'd like to contribute and for joining us in this way on such a special day!

Then I added a postscript:

> After writing this email, Gmail auto-filled its suggestion for the subject line: Christmas performance! Kind of?! Here's hoping it's a five-star event with not too many plot twists!

The songs that came back were vibrant and varied, a smattering of Taylor Swift's *Evermore* album and reimagined lullabies, rhythmic blues, and walk-up power anthems. I loved it immediately, and the playlist became my soundtrack for labor prep workouts. With their help, I soon discovered staying with my breath was greatly supported by song. My sister Allison suggested Joseph's "Blood and Tears," noting, "Okay, maybe this isn't the *best* title for your impending situation, but I love these lyrics: 'If it'll be a fight regardless, I only want the fight to be with you.'"

I also found a grounding force in renewing the rituals of the season we had forgone for so long. One night, Zach and I hauled the ornament boxes up from the basement that hadn't been unpacked in a decade. Since we hadn't lived near family until then, we'd always traveled for half of December, and opted out of doing our own tree because it didn't seem practical. We unboxed ornaments that I had inherited from my grandmother that still smelled like her house. We strung up Zach's baby footprints, cinnamon dough ornaments that our parents had arguably kept too long, and globes with dates and photos from Christmases past. All of these were both familiar and forgotten, like finding something precious that had been lost—a locket found in the floorboards, a wedding photo tucked into a book.

We put on the Christmas albums from our childhoods as we fixed the last of the ornaments up on the tree, then crowned the top with the tin star I got Zach for our tenth anniversary. We knew we were pregnant then, in late May, and we knew my Christmastide due date, and I couldn't wait then to be where we were now: so close to meeting our girl.

We will remember that evening as a time of nostalgia greeting the new. We were claiming these traditions as our own now. With an excess of Christmas lights left over, Zach said, "Maybe I'll deck out the porch. I don't know, maybe get one of those giant wreaths."

"A *wreath*?" I laughed.

He laughed right back at me, watching how I wobbled on tiptoe to reach the top branches.

I have always known Zach to be either a holdout or all in. To him, anything that is worth doing is worth overdoing, or not at all. It was incredible to see him like this: gone soft before a tangle of twinkly lights, going all in on his joy. Our daughter wasn't even here yet and she was already showing me a new side of him. And I loved what I saw.

One week before my due date, mid-December, I woke early, 5 A.M., with a light tugging gathering force, and when it was a decent hour to call the doctor I did. I was patched through to their off-hours line and a male doctor answered, which surprised me, since the reason I chose this clinic was because it had all-women doctors.

"Is this your first?" A question I still don't know how to answer. But for what he needed to know, I said yes. "It could be a while, then. Tomorrow, or even in a few days. Call us when the contractions are five minutes apart." This was not the news I wanted to hear.

Through breakfast, a hot shower, and a morning of compulsive googling while Zach channeled his own nerves cleaning the house top to bottom, the pulsing cramps stayed with me. I had to take breaks and sit on the cold tile while blow-drying my hair. In retrospect, I could tell they were building, but the hot water and steam of the shower obscured the sensation from me. Even so, I felt discouraged and a little scared, since I kept reading that early labor starts in the back then gathers around the front.

I had worked hard to build up my strength. Yet if this was just early labor, the mere preamble for the "real" pain ahead, I didn't know if I could do it.

I had been texting my mom updates throughout the day, and around dinnertime, after twelve hours of this, she asked how I was doing.

"Kind of the same?" I said. "Definitely rhythmic back pain but still not in front at all."

"I never had labor in front," she said, and she'd done this three times. "I always had back labor."

This was the first time it occurred to me that this might really be happening, we might really be progressing after all. By sunset, I was on my elliptical, walking through what I now knew was showtime and advancing contractions. As evening fell, things got more intense. I set up the heat pad on the couch and cued up *Gilmore Girls*, a throwback comfort show for me. The Christmas tree lights and their reflection in the window became my focal point, their brightness my steadiness. And then, when Lorelai was stuck at the spa with her mother, who'd just scheduled them for a couples massage, my water broke in a great burst.

Speaking of her own labor, Louise Erdrich described how her husband found her on the floor in a posture "of furious prayer."[11] And that's where I found myself then: hands and knees on my yoga mat, Zach's hands on my hips providing the support of counterpressure, the dog starting to panic and circle us anxiously.

"Birth is intensely spiritual and physical all at once," Erdrich writes. "The contractions do not stop. There is no giving up this physical prayer."[12]

Not thirty minutes later, I was in my hospital gown and the doctor I had spoken to on the phone earlier was saying, "All right, you're nine centimeters dilated." And then, in the best news I could have heard in that moment: "You should be ready to push within the hour." He smiled. "I guess those back pains really were something after all!" Later I would learn he was the owner of the ob-gyn practice, formerly the chief of staff of this very maternity ward.

In my mind, contractions will always be circular: the rise, crest, and return of tension, arcing again and again, tight and small at first then large and all encompassing. As they swept me into their orbit, each circle held the history of everything: every tension I've ever known, every fevered pain, blessed downshift and release, moment of peace, and here we go again. The night was dark and in it everything went radial, cycling through rhythms of pressure and release.

You can take nothing with you into labor, except your breath. And right now, as pain raked deep nerve, and hips locked in hot spasm, my breath was the only mercy I had carrying me from moment to moment:

Inhale: *I AM*

Exhale: *With Us*

I asked for a squat bar, as I found that what my body wanted was to be in an active position. So when I felt the next wave coming, I would tell Zach and the nurse and hoist myself up on the bar with their support. What I remember: how every muscle strained to hold me up, up, up; how Zach's hands firmly anchored mine as I gripped the bar; how his solidness steadied me. How my "calm focus" playlist sounded its benedictions over my pain and assured me I was not alone in this.

I am beloved, I am baptized, I am badass.

I kept my eyes closed most of the time. At one point, Zach asked me, "Do you want me to tie your hair back?" noticing my pandemic-grown-long hair swinging fast and low as the contractions quickened. He had snapped a hair tie on his wrist before leaving for the hospital, just for me, and I don't know that I've felt more loved.

Still, I said no. By then I was deep in the elsewhere, and I needed to stay wild.

They call it transition when a woman's labor pains reach their peak like a fever breaking. This is the moment of reckoning, when words like "I can't" are cried, when self-doubt spikes into sickening altitude, but it's also the surest signal that she's almost through.

The nurse said, "We can see her head! Do you want to feel it?" I did not. Time blurred wordless, searing at the edges. Language had left me long ago. I knew she was coming; I didn't need the proof of touch to believe. I just needed to stay in my fight to get her here. I think that's when I started roaring.

It was her hand that came out first—a tiny star that burst forth fisting and waving. Then the crescendo in the room: *You're doing it! Almost there!* And then—*and then*—two of the most beautiful words I know—a rush and tumble from my body, a felt surrender, and the *I AM, With Us* rhythm that had carried me made sudden way for *She Is.*

In my memory, it happened so fast. Someone lifted her up and over toward me and she was a sun rising, the spectacle of her being a planet in accelerated ascent. She landed on my chest with a cry and suddenly, after so much, we were here: skin on skin in this wide sleeve of night, warmed by the hot astonishment of our belonging.

In that moment, I was every mother who had ever loved: magnetized to her presence, the majesty of her being, staring into the sun.

Her whole tiny body was blush red, her hair dark and wet. Her eyes midnight deep, their blue searching for mine. We named her Quinn, meaning wise queen, Quinn Shiloh, meaning peace. Pain, once absolute, was now simply a house cat that snuck out the back door, having given its quiet concession to past tense, overshadowed completely by presence.

Psychiatrist Curt Thompson writes of this primary human need, "We all are born into the world looking for someone looking for us, and . . . we remain in this mode of searching for the rest of our lives."[13]

We are all searching for the face of love, for the presence that has made room for us.

We dare not call it basic. This labor is Advent, it is arrival, it is downright spiritual—as are all labors of love.

"I've seen a lot of newborns," the nurse said, tucking Quinn back into my arms after the newborn tests and weight were taken. "But this one takes the cake for being one of the cutest," which of course delighted me. Zach would later insist she said this to every new mother, and like every new mother, I would deny this. I asked her to take our picture, our first as the three of us, and it was only when she handed my phone back to me and I saw it that I realized I still had my mask on. I had never taken it off.

Finally came my wheelchair trip down the hall to our maternity suite, where I went to plug in my phone and found the battery at 1 percent. My playlist had held and carried me through the contractions, the pushing, the long-awaited golden hour. It had been just enough. In the deepest physical pain of my life, I had been held.

It was in the early morning hours and I was certainly spent, but it was like my body did not know how to come down from that kind of adrenaline. I was overjoyed, enchanted, yet shook for hours. While Zach tucked up on the converted window seat bed, I just kept looking at her in the bassinet thinking, *I am responsible for this tiny person's space, time, matter.* Thinking, *Love has come through my body and now I am looking right at her.* Her beginning, as small as a grain of hourglass sand. Yet after, her being, her multitudes, wide as the night that held us both.

It was Advent's week of joy. My first experience of motherhood was absence, one year ago this very week. Now it was presence. The love of both will stay with me for life.

Poet Kamand Kojouri writes, "The greatest moments in our lives occur when we surrender: birth, love, and death."[14] That first night, I don't think I slept at all—stretching still, to take it all in.

The next day came the first true snow of the season. The snow fell all day in gentle anointing while we ate our reconstituted eggs and sipped coffee from hospital Styrofoam, met with lactation consultants, and held and held a sleeping Quinn.

It might have been lovely, except I had lost a lot of blood, to the point that I had to have medical interventions to prevent postpartum hemorrhaging. I had sustained greater birth injuries than I had expected. I hadn't slept in over thirty-six hours. And the baby was losing too much weight. So tiny and new, she kept falling asleep when she was supposed to be feeding, so our care team put us on a two-hour feeding regimen, day and night.

The first day it was well into the afternoon and I still hadn't slept, unable to nap all day—my adrenaline still fizzing—when finally a nurse said to me, "Do you feel like you've been hit by a truck?" and I immediately thought it was brilliant and compassionate of her not to say, "You *look* like you've been hit by a truck."

And yes, it hurt to walk to the bathroom, hurt to pee, hurt to sit up, hurt just to be, all the while worrying about Quinn not eating and slipping toward "failure to thrive."

"We need to get you to sleep," the nurse said. It was not a question. And I knew we had a long night ahead of us, waking every two hours to try again and again.

We wouldn't have made it without the help of the nursing staff. After nine months of quarantine, void of the small civilities of small talk, check-out conversations, sidewalk hellos, their kindness was like being lifted out of sensory deprivation. Chantelle sang her name like a bell every time she entered the room to bring me fresh ice and check my vitals. Jessica went on a hospital-wide hunt to find me some Earl Grey tea when I asked if they had any.

The care of touch and simple human courtesy were gifts I didn't know I had needed so desperately until I received them. How long had it been since I had made eye contact with someone who was not my husband, my blood relative? Even without the full-range subtleties of human expression concealed behind their masks, those three days in the hospital were to date the most social event of our year. In the greatest physical recovery of my life, it was the pure unmerited compassion of strangers toward my body that saved me.

Those first days were like a snow globe: just as gorgeous, just as fragile—for is there anything more vulnerable than a newborn? So much skin on skin, snow on snow.

We were discharged on the third afternoon, after Quinn's weight was deemed stable enough. A snowstorm was coming and they wanted to get us home before it came. So we dressed Quinn in a pinecone onesie and gold velvet headband and drove home at the blue hour of dusk. Since the snow had fallen, the streets were empty and all was quiet, illuminated only by the streetlights and Christmas lights on the houses. This is the memory Zach and I will hold for a lifetime, because for 1.9 miles between the hospital and a houseful of family ready to receive us, it was the three of us, our new forever normal. Because for 1.9 miles, driving ten miles per hour with precious cargo, taking in the quiet glamour of a snowfallen city after so great an ordeal, the world seemed gentle.

My parents met us at the door, giddy and already quibbling about who would get to hold her first. "Meet Quinn," we said. We hugged for the first time in a year, since last Christmas, since my last postpartum when we did not bring the baby home. And we were ushered back into the communion of touch.

Life is full of contractions, cycles of rising and releasing tension, the pain of transition, the weary thrill of coming through. These are rhythms not just of labor, but human rhythms of life itself.

But it must be said there comes a moment where the metaphor breaks. Labor pain is unique in that it is pain as passageway—as much as the contractions hurt, they are the wisdom of the body at work, a body that knows what it is designed to do, a body that is fighting to soon see a face. It's pain, but the pain is proof that the body is *working* and life is on its way.

But most pain is not like this. The snap of bone, slip on black ice, seeing stars through splitting headaches—this is pain that shouts, *Something is wrong.* A laboring woman's transition might be known as breakthrough pain, but most of the time, pain simply breaks. And even birth, as we know, does not always lead to the life we'd hoped for.

What I mean to say is there is no inherent virtue in suffering. We are loved by a God who suffers with us, but makes no mandates about what measure of pain we must endure as a method of righteous-making. As we ache for our bodies, our communities, our world to be made right, Advent makes space for our ache and declares it sacred to God. This, too, is Incarnation: God rushing to be with us in our hurt.

After we'd spent so much time in tight quarantine, our Christmas was a full-out, monthlong house party. Our families generously made sacrifices of time and convenience to quarantine and test so we could gather safely, and we lived it large: the campiest Christmas sweaters, holiday cocktail contests, huge steaming pans of mac and cheese and hearty stews, all the while marveling at the newest member.

My dad pronounces her eyes are midnight blue. My sister says her blinks are like a grand plié, in slow, elegant ballet. Her belly button is a perfect rosette. Her cheeks are velvet, especially against mine. She lives with her knees bunched up and out, creating a little heart with her body. I have a photo of her in this pose in her berry-red pajamas and she looks the picture of a valentine. No one can get over how beautiful she is.

Holding her while I'm about to shower one day, my sister Rebecca says, "It's like watching a bonfire. Not that it's riveting exactly, but you just can't stop looking." How can something so brightly alive be at the same time so tranquil?

It has been said that every child is an incarnation. And she is ours: so much hope, now here in the flesh.

She is so quintessentially Quinn that I feel the prick of sorrow to know there was another who was just as much wholly her own.

And then I remember the labor does not end with the delivery. The work of the womb is far from over after the birth. The contractions of a mother circle for a lifetime, radiating love in surge and plummet in response to her beloved. Suffering-with, grieving-with, celebrating-with, her love forever now a bond of sacred preposition. Such profound *with-ness* will always stretch a person, as we make room for the experiences of another within ever-expanding human empathy.

Theologian Elizabeth Johnson writes, "When God is spoken of as merciful, the semantic tenor of the word indicates that the womb is trembling, yearning for the child, grieved at the pain."[15]

Nothing makes the most powerful muscle in the human body tremble like love. And this love will never stop laboring on behalf of her beloved. This may be the most primal declaration Advent has to make.

On December 21, the winter solstice again, Zach and I remembered our bonfire of lament a year past, and we lit a candle for her at dinner with my family, after Quinn had gone to sleep. There were tears around the table, especially my mom's, who tucked a card into my hand later reading, in the way of the Quaker prayer tradition, "Even on the darkest night, we hold you in the light. We look with you toward the final Advent, when we will meet her at last."

Advent is the waiting for so abstract a hope to become flesh. It is the practiced hope of a world made right and whole again. We, as a people, are waiting. How long will we have to wait for life to have the last word? How long will our love tremble? Who can say?

For tonight, we remembered the darkness of loss, and we lit a candle toward the future in which we shall meet. And our daughter slept upstairs in peace.

Maybe her incarnation will reclaim, stake down, some of the timelessness that we had lost. Maybe the time of birth, the particularities of pounds and ounces, the syllables of her name, the cadence of her cries will consecrate time anew, reclaim it from the blur, the desecrated hours and months and years that had been that year, give us the immeasurable gift of a bright line beginning.

Advent is, after all, an origin story. What better way to mark time than to call it, to declare this is it: the beginning of a story you are going to love.

GOING GENTLY INTO THE NEW

Epiphany, Again

I AM the way of the soft, slow, and steady
With You in the tension of the now and the not-yet

In this tension, this both/and, we love and move and have
our being, all in the presence of a God who also sobs and
sings.

AMANDA EVANS OPELT, *A Hole in the World*

"Does your doctor know how many stairs are in your house?"
my mom had asked me a month or so before my due
date, her brow creasing with concern. We lived in a tall, skinny
row house in Olde Uptown, with wondrously tall ceilings and
two flights all the way to the top where my office is perched like
a treehouse. And I scoffed ever so slightly and thought, How is
that possibly medically relevant? My body was about to do something magnificent; surely it could handle a flight or two of stairs.
I'd take them slow! But she knew then what I had yet to learn:
just how leveling postpartum—the after—can be.

If Advent heralds new beginnings, the spirit of Epiphany is transition. Time as we know it is creased upon the fold line of Christ's

birth, dividing history into Before Christ and After. And Epiphany commences this season of the After.

But it begins, if we take a closer look, in the thick of Mary's postpartum. This seems right to me. In this intensely vulnerable time, the mother of God was like all mothers: Her body was in need of recovery, her sleep was disrupted, her hormones were surging, her sense of self no doubt shaken, her system surely in overload.

We might even say Epiphany is the postpartum era of a world reborn: just as tenuous, just as wondrous, just as new.

Mary had never had a baby before, and God had never been born before. The first Epiphany held the vulnerability of a newborn God, a postpartum teenager, and an entire world reborn into a new age. It held recovery, adjustment, and transition, both writ small and writ large. And it extends ancient wisdom to us in our transitions, small and large, today.

New beginnings are beautiful, but even the celebration of the new can hold the grief of change. Moving to a new home means leaving an old home, perhaps an old community, behind. Starting a new job can carry bitter with the sweet. Celebrating a milestone birthday can carry excitement and gratitude as well as the unease of aging. I will long remember my little sister's wedding day as one of the happiest days of my life, and yet between the ceremony and the sunflower-studded reception, I broke out in hives. At first, I could not understand why, but later realized this was "happy stress"—my body's way of processing so tectonic a change, even if a celebrated one.

I have come to love this particular season in the Christian year because Epiphany is an invitation to be gentle with ourselves in the tender space of transition. To acknowledge that it is not so easy to become something that we've never been before. It is not so easy to be reborn.

Forget the stairs. As it turns out, I could barely make it down the hall.

Three days postpartum, we had to take Quinn to the pediatrician's office for another weight check, to make sure she wasn't losing any more. Zach drove and carried in the car seat, and all I had to do was take the steps into the building, hop onto the elevator, and walk down the hall to the suite. The only problem was the hall was as long as a runway, and walking sent shooting hot stars of pain all over my body. As empowering as my birth experience was, I had sustained significant personal injuries, and I felt them with every step. Just yesterday, they had escorted me out of the hospital in a wheelchair. And now I was just supposed to . . . bounce back? I winced at the thought of it. There would definitely not be any bouncing.

Zach knew I was struggling and tried to handle the check-in so I wouldn't have to. "We're here for Dr. Allen."

"Excellent!" said the woman behind the Plexiglas. She had bright purple cat-eye glasses and a cloud of white cumulus hair. Surely someone's grandmother, surely someone who remembered not just birthdays but half birthdays, who had snacks on her person at all times.

I was already looking at my shoes, already trying not to cry from the physical exertion. "Aren't *you* something," she said to Quinn, beaming.

Then to Zach, "All right then, and she must be Mom," and flourished a set of papers for us to fill out.

And suddenly there it was, the moment I'd been bracing for long before Quinn had ever been born.

Of course I was a mom now. Of course I was so much *more* than a mom. This kind stranger was making no suggestion otherwise. But in the rawness of my state, in hearing this new name before I was ready for it, I misheard it as the proclamation that this is *all* you are now.

I sobbed the entire drive home in the passenger seat. I told Zach, "I don't know why I'm crying." I didn't have the words to name it then, but I do now.

Names are sacred, new ones especially, and in the vulnerability of being newly born myself, I had not yet made the space needed to choose to take this one on for myself. "Mother" is a powerful identity to bear, a word spring-loaded with fierce joy and protective rage, mixed baggage and multitudes, which is too heavy a coronation to be awarded without one's consent. And even then, such a name takes time to grow into.

I would have a lifetime ahead of me in this new name and never would it hold the electric charge it did for me that day. But at the time, I hated that I had been renamed without my consent, that this woman spoke to my husband as if I wasn't standing right there, as if I wasn't a human who belonged to myself. But did I? With just a few words, I felt as if I had been relegated: Yesterday you were your own with a name of your own, but today and henceforth forevermore you are known only to the world via adjacency.

This is what I believe: Love always makes more of a person, not less. Anyone who classifies a woman as "just a mom" is grossly mistaken. "Just" is diminutive and it is absurd to attempt to make small of a woman whose interior life is expanding like the universe itself.

And yet, many women are made to feel less in their personhood because they have chosen to make more space for others through parenthood. For nine months, a woman's body is tended to, checked up on, cared for, and then when the baby on her insides comes out, it is a common experience to feel demoted to caregiver instead of someone worthy of care themselves. As her first-person personhood is reduced to a third-person reference, it is easy to feel her existence is only validated as accessory to the miracle of someone else's life.

I had become a parent, which I wanted deeply, but I still wanted to be a person, too. And I was so steeped in the idea that only men get to be both simultaneously.

We observe this assumption in the colloquial category of "working moms," but rarely if ever the counterpart "working dads." This assumption goes unspoken in the routine installation of diaper changers in women's restrooms but rarely men's. We see it in the public perception of a man pushing his toddler on the park swings who must be "Dad of the Year," while a woman parenting at the playground is "just a mom." And we see it in the public crediting of men who leave the workplace early to "cover" for their wife while their women colleagues are frowned upon for clocking in late because of a rough drop-off that morning.

It seemed to me that any woman who had children became "Mom" by default in any setting, the precursor to her personhood and any public identifier. But a man with kids was simply who he always was, until "Dad Duty" came calling in neat tidy segments of time.

I wanted this baby. I wanted this togetherness. I wanted to still be me. And I didn't want this to be too much to ask.

In the first forty days postpartum, midwives call this interpersonal closeness the "Motherbaby." In these early days, the two are one; there is no separation between them.

My Epiphany brought a new revelation, a new name, a new transformation—indeed, everything I had hoped for, made all the more meaningful after our experience of loss. I was still me, but my daughter and I were now a dyad, and the intensity of this togetherness, of need and self-giving, would take some getting used to.

In those first few months, Quinn was obsessed with finding the edges of a thing, always reaching for the end of the yoga mat, the rug, the satin trim of her blanket, the curve of my clavicle, the edge of me. "Give me the edges of the world," Zach says of her. Yet while she contented herself with discovering them, I crashed gracelessly against mine.

I had just gone from being a woman power walking through late-stage labor to a woman who could not walk herself to the bathroom without the banister's support. I had long fancied myself as the high-capacity type, yet I had become a person whose life was confined between a bed and a donut pillow. I had gone from being a person who Handles Things to a person who asked and asked and asked for help. I was living in whiplash: the snap of succession from power to powerlessness.

This was my postpartum revelation: It wasn't labor and delivery that leveled me, it was what came *after*. It wasn't labor that pushed me to cry "I can't do this," it was the postpartum immersion, the place where I said it again and again, *I can't do this*. Again and again in this tender season of epiphany, I was astonished at just how limited I was postbirth, and for how long. Everything was jagged, everything was visceral. It was not helping things that I kept pushing against the frayed edges of my finitude, which was perhaps a muddled attempt at penance for some unspoken part of me that wondered if I was allowed to struggle. If I *deserved* to struggle receiving the very gift I so deeply wanted.

And that was before I came down with a double ear infection. It was so bad that at my six-week checkup, at which I was not yet healed, I told my doctor it was a toss-up whether this or actual labor was more painful. And I meant it.

I remembered the woman who gave birth to my daughter, the woman who let her hair swing wild, who roared. Where was she now? Had she left us? I needed her strength more than ever.

Writer Sinéad Gleeson writes, "Pain is about answering a question the body asks."[1] And my body was asking me in neon: *Will you honor your limits?*

For many years, I had answered my body, *Limits? What are those?* For many years, I had marched under the banner of pushing through. I was the insufferable person who brought my laptop to my salon appointments, typing away on deadline while my highlights set in their foils. I worked weekends because I thought I had to, and took calls from bosses and business partners on West Coast time late into the evenings. One time a massage therapist counted twenty-six knots studded in my shoulder blades. Many times, my body's question went unanswered.

In my birth prep program, one instructor walked through exercise modifications for mamas. "You have to respect your range of motion," she said. "Pushing yourself will not make your healing go faster. It will only get you hurt."

This was my new range of motion. My capacity had been radically redefined. I was faced with the choice we all have when confronted with our limitations: We can either fight our limited capacity and twist the screw, or make our peace with it and so make space for our healing to begin.

Pushing through is not a great life strategy, of course. In a purely physical sense, if you overload your core, you will only weaken it. Overload your life, and it will only weaken your interior foundations. Pushing through a relationship that is not working, a job that is asking far more than any one person can give, an obligation you wish you hadn't said yes to, or self-imposed impossible standards will not "get the job done"; it will deplete your vital systems and put you at risk of getting hurt.

If I truly believe the circle of the liturgical year is big enough to hold every high and low, then I am pressed to accept that it is big enough to hold my fragility, too. If I truly want to live expansively, making room for life's polarities of love, loss, and liminality, then I am pressed to accept that limits are part of this sacred story. The father of Israel walked away from his sacred encounter with God with a new name, but also a limp. Angels attended prophets in the wilderness with food and water because even God could see that "the journey is too much" (1 Kings 19:7). The Psalms speak of strength sapped and bones wasting away; the parables, of bodies in hunger and thirst, in need of shelter. Even Jesus honored his own human limitations by slipping out the back to be alone when the crowds became too much and too many.

If I wanted to heal, I was going to have to stop fighting my finitude and let it live alongside the rest.

Counterintuitively, there is freedom in such acceptance of our finitude. If we are limitless, how quickly this slips into becoming *beholden*. If we are limitless, we are on the hook to make the most of our own power at all times (how exhausting). Yet drawing an honest line around what we can do, separating from what we cannot, sets us free.

If our capacity is a circle, no matter how small or how large, we can spend our lives fighting its edges, or we can survey our spheres honestly, accept the space that is ours, and perhaps find some joy there. We can either respect our range of motion, or empty our energies bracing and crashing against that which we cannot change. Ultimately, accepting our limits is the humbling practice of self-forgiveness, as we let go of the notion that we should be stronger than we are or have more capacity than we do.

Drawing this honest line might even unfold new capacities within us, as getting up close and personal with our limitations opens up new channels of empathy for ourselves and for others.

One evening after Quinn was finally down, I texted my friend a photo of me—bundled in my bathrobe on the toilet, with a towel tented over my head. "If you need me," I said, "I'll be right here." I was soaking in an Epsom salt sitz bath and cupping a mug of steaming hot water toward my throbbing ears. She texted back a GIF of someone spitting out their coffee laughing. "What am I looking at?"

"My new normal. My new capacity," I wrote back. "Maybe healing." It's not a pretty picture. But it's a true one. Accepting our limits is one of the truest stories that can be told, and there is some peace in this, even if it's of the scruffy sort.

Maybe it wasn't a terrible place to be, after all, making peace with the edges of my capacity. Respecting my range of motion. Honoring my limits. Far from healed, but on my way.

Her skin is sweet cream, her body a moon crescent, and I am her sky.

While time before her was measured in wide, open fields of waiting, now it is marked by hairpin-tight turns of magnificent need. Her body is in constant communion with mine. My body becomes a metronome, a tick tick tick of time, set for every two to three hours, day and night. This is our shared liturgy: ticktock, take and eat, my body a cup that fills and empties itself again and again, for her.

Angela Garbes writes, "Christians are taught that Jesus Christ once turned water into wine. Around the world, women's bodies perform a similar miracle, every hour, every day."[2] A body creating milk ex nihilo is surely a miracle, yet the constancy of this process can also border on the maddening.

Nights are splintered by supply and demand, desperate rituals of consolation in the dark. Meaghan O'Connell writes that those early postpartum days are like being dropped into an ongoing emergency. "Endure the car crash of birth, then, without sleeping, use your broken body to keep your tiny, fragile, precious, heartbreaking mortal child alive."[3] Something like that, yes.

Can you imagine it: the heaviness of a human body hurled

against you night after night, at all hours, inconsolable in what can only be interpreted as grief. It makes no difference that this particular body belongs to an infant. A baby is not a separate category from human.

It wasn't just my body that felt its limits; I felt the push and pull in deeper parts of me. To be with her now, to take in her every detail, after losing and waiting and hoping for so long, is a superlative of joy. This is also true: The whiplash, the metaphysical shock, the supreme need crashing into my most vulnerable state is enough to take anyone to the brink.

And even still: Her skin is sweet cream, her body a moon crescent, and I am her sky.

This love is a paradox, big enough to hold a universe of both/and.

Her presence radiates with a magnetic force I am constantly drawn toward. And in it there is also a death; I do not feel like I belong to myself. Every hour holds bliss, boredom, oblivion. As one writer puts it, "It is lovely; it is intolerable; it is both."[4]

Our world had never been wider. The life Zach and I have shared together had been a closed circle for a decade; now it unfolds to make space for another. Though it was also true that our world had never been smaller: We'd rarely left our house or had outside contact besides family, doctors, and the occasional grocery cashier, for the better part of a year. In the past twelve months, we filled up our gas tank four times.

Our December held two daughters: one we were constantly holding, and one we never got to touch, and we experienced this as both love and lament. I had never felt such transcendence, nor such tedium. My body and time had never felt more limited. These realities jostled each other hour by hour in constant dissonant duet.

I read one mother's account, "Motherhood is a relentless,

humbling toggle between fortitude and surrender, recognizing the power I possess and then coming to terms again with how quickly it can be bled away."[5]

What is a person supposed to do with this kind of push and pull? How are any of us supposed to live in such paradox?

Even then, I knew the answer, though I resisted it. Paradox cannot be mastered like a puzzle, solved for x. Ultimately, the only way to endure paradox is to make our peace with it, accepting the tension of its terms for what they are. Shauna Niequist writes, "A wise friend of mine says that true spiritual maturity is nothing more—and nothing less—than consenting to reality."[6]

This was my reality: My body was broken and I was no longer certain that I belonged to myself. This was my range of motion: mostly bedrest, asking for help, taking it slow. And this was my choice: I could either bring injury upon myself fighting my limits in defiant denial, or make my peace with the paradox and consent to reality already.

Thresholds always bring paradox, because they always divide between the before and the after. And perhaps both the gift and the bracing of Epiphany comes in the way that it brings paradox to light in our lives. We spend so much restless energy here, afraid to step over. We are skittish about leaving what we know, moving forward into what we don't. So we straddle the line.

There is a ready language for making our peace with the paradox embedded in our spiritual practice already, should we attend to it. We find this word at the end of most prayers in four unfussy letters: *amen*. This word originated in ancient Israel, when it was declared collectively by the people in response to hearing the word of God. The word is derived from the Hebrew verb meaning "to be trusted" or "to be reliable," and Jesus repeated this word seventy-seven times in the Gospels as a signal of emphasis and truth telling, something that "had no parallel in Jewish practice."[7]

Then in Revelation, Jesus himself is referred to as "the Amen" (3:14), the realest real, the truest true.

Amen is a way of saying, "This is true. And so it is. And may it be so." This simple word spans the distance of the spiritual journey by naming what is, what we hope will be, and recognizing God's presence with us in the in-between. It offers us honest expression of both naming the rawness of our reality and voicing our desperate hope for change, all the while affirming that God is with us in the tension between.

Perhaps this one word expresses the spirit of Epiphany: The good, glorious news is that the one we've been waiting for has come! But the world has not been made new, not just yet. Emmanuel is God with us, yet his presence does not instantly do away with the present pain, death, powers of empire. Advent is a beginning—both of the church year and of a world made new—but it is far from resolution.

This tension is so palpable and precise that theologians have named it: We live in the already-not-yet.

Death has been undone in Christ. He is the one declaring, "I am making everything new!" (Revelation 21:5). Yet the making takes time, and the new is still unfolding. The church lives its life in the meantime between the now and the not yet, resurrection amid our broken reality and its fullest fulfillment at the end of time as we know it.

Epiphany, perhaps more than any other season, teaches us how to inhabit the tension of the now-not-yet. There is no glittering triumphalism here, only the tender early days of a world reborn, a life made new, and through it all, the call to go gently. The permission to be in process as we wait and long to be made whole.

I think of how Jesus taught us to pray: "Your kingdom come, your will be done, on earth as it is in heaven" (Matthew 6:10).

Certainly earth's reality is a far cry from heaven's, and this prayer to me models that even as we accept the terms of our current conditions, we can pray and hope and fight for a better world. In this way, *amen* might be our one-word practice of making peace with the paradox of living. Because for now, paradox is where we live.

God is in the whiplash of our before and afters.

God is in the push-and-pull of our desires, uncertainties, and constraints.

God is in the paradox of our most empowered moments and our most leveling limitations.

Amen. And so it is. And may it be so.

Amen: We consent to the paradox, we affirm God is in even this.

This is my reality: broken sleep, broken body, shuffled sense of self, and spending my days with the most beautiful human snuggled on my chest, heart to heart. Here is astonishing limitation, here is beauty. Here is paradox. Here is God.

A cold morning in late January, I tried to voice this simple prayer.

I should have recovered by now, or so I felt, since I had passed the six-week mark so often touted as the universal healing period (though even the medical community is nuancing this now). But I had only just evolved beyond bedrest. Quinn should have been getting the hang of her days and nights by now, but she had been up the night before at two, three, four. I checked the weather— eight degrees out. The rickety old radiators were hissing trying to keep up. I didn't want to begin another day defeated.

It was far too cold for a baby outdoors, but something in me suddenly craved the open air, after so much winter cocooning.

"You should go," Zach said, bringing me strong, black coffee. "I've got our girl."

I indulged the notion and bundled up to my nose for a walk, which wasn't so much of a walk as it was a three-block excursion down to see the river (in the limits of my new capacity, I knew better than to go much farther). My world had been so small for so long. I suppose I wanted a wider view.

What I wasn't prepared for was the view itself. The Susquehanna is one of the oldest river systems in the world, more ancient than even the Nile. Like any river, its one constant through the ages is its current. But today, in this record cold, its rushing had simply *stopped*—from bank to bank, the water had frozen over.

The river's stillness was striking, its usual mile-wide motion slowed to silent ice. All that sun-glinted snow and ice formation—it was beautiful. To behold it was to hear what most of us are not brave enough to say out loud: Even for the river, there is a time to be still.

If the Susquehanna could surrender to winter's rest for a time, trusting that in the turning of the seasons she would flow free again, maybe I could, too.

I was barely a week postpartum when the algorithms started coming for me with their imperatives to "get my body back," dangling seven-step, three-payment programs promising to help me do just that. It's a curious pitch, really: Give us your money to pretend that nine months of your life and an unprecedented bodily experience never happened. My body had not even stopped bleeding yet.

Then as pandemic variants rose and fell like rolling waves, this imperative echoed anew: We just have to "get back to normal." As if millions of lives had not been lost, as if the traumas of isolation and fear have not shaped us. As if the years of enduring all that we've endured can simply be erased in favor of an ever-glittering future.

Maybe your "before" and "after" is a painful threshold—the fracturing of a relationship, the hard no when you hoped for a yes, the death of a loved one you can't imagine a future without. And you're feeling the pressure to "get over it," to get "back to normal."

But the implicit ask embedded within this mindset is to *pretend what stretched you never happened.* Just hit "undo" and pretend the pain never happened. Just pretend the enduring, the deepening, the becoming were simply pages you could rip out of the book.

Whether postpartum or postpandemic or post- any life-shaping event, there is no going back to normal in the After. As if it could be possible to erase everything that has happened since. We've seen too much. We've seen death and life and maybe even some resurrection. But even the resurrection does not dare pretend that death did not happen, that death was not also part of its story.

I think of this with some comfort: At the kingdom come, we will be welcomed by a God whose very body bears the immutable memory of pain. The scars of Christ descended into hell, rose on the third day, ascended into heaven, and in the eschaton, all our scars will come with us. Mothers will have their stretch marks, their C-section scars, their intimate scars. Grown-ups will have echoes of childhood knee scrapes and bike tumbles on their skin, scabs we shouldn't have picked at, but did anyway. And we will all have scars of the unseen variety, the wounds that never broke skin but nevertheless struck deep. Our scars, seen and unseen, will remain, and may even be the only thing we take with us into a new age.

Our skin tells the story of what we've been through. Scars mark the spot where something very real happened, right here, that cannot be erased. And they tell the story of our healing.

Because resurrection is real, but it is not erasure. It is not some cosmic undo button for the suffering that has come before. It is not a slate wiped clean, a cold lobotomy, a canceling out. Resurrection is only real if death, too, is real. God in Jesus remembers what it is like to die—to encounter the certainty that comes with the final breath in knowing the end is now. Death does not have the last word, but it does leave its mark, even on God. Jesus lives, but he lives with scars, both on his body and within his memory. Theologian Nancy Eiesland goes so far as to say that as the risen Christ opens his scarred palms to the disciples, "this disabled God is . . . the revealer of a new humanity."[8]

The body does not forget all that has happened. Our scars are memory keepers.

Erasure is not an option. Our bodies have seen too much.

The postpartum journey is about vulnerability, healing, and ultimately rejoining the world, yet never as before. My body has scars that tell stories I'm immensely proud of. Erase that? Hell, no. To take from me my own transformation would be too great a loss. I'd rather my body remember her strength, and I'd rather her strength remember me.

Whether a birth or a death or the whiplash of the unexpected, true healing after any intense before-and-after event will never come through "bouncing back." The story of the healing we need will never be one of bouncing back, but one of humaning through. In fact, the mandate to get *back* to normal as quickly as possible is perhaps the greatest interference to our healing, which cannot be rushed. No pain can heal without acknowledgment; but there is no pain that cannot be healed through the very same. To go *back* is the definition of regression. But there is no going back to who we were before, undoing all we have endured. There is only the slow, daily work of living forward into our healing.

My friend KJ went through a period of hospitalizations as her body kept going into anaphylactic shock, without any answers yet as to why. Between systemic inflammation and the effects of high-dose steroids, her body and face became, in her own words, unrecognizable to her.

The first time she noticed the widening of her face, how foreign she looked to herself, she happened upon a photo of her younger sister in her camera roll. At first glance, the photo shows a smiling young adult, fresh off a magical ride at Disney World. At second glance, her face is as wide as KJ's is now, her body seated in a wheelchair. This was no ordinary vacation. Their parents had decided to take the trip as a celebration that their daughter had survived a lupus-induced heart attack at twenty years old, just months before.

That face was so very like the face she now beheld in her own reflection, flaring a thousand unanswered questions. "That face," KJ thought, "means she survived." She looked herself straight in the eye of that hospital mirror, cupped her face in her hands, and resolved: "This shape means you are surviving."

In a health update, KJ confessed how I imagine most of us feel about the hard gift of honoring our limitations:

"The shape of survival is softer than I wish. It is harder to see, and more humbling to let be seen. And essential. From my face to my frustrations, there is a softness to survival that, when I allow myself to be witnessed with acceptance and attention, becomes a thin and holy place."[9]

And in beholding herself and her own softness that night, a bathroom mirror became such a holy place.

If the resurrected Christ lives with the jagged skin of scars, surely we can make space for our own vulnerabilities to belong among all the rest. Surely we can look our softness straight in the eye and see it as the strength of our survival. After all, vulnerability is just another way of saying your humanity is showing. Your only-humanness is showing. So I say let it show.

The thing about scars is that they itch when they heal. This, too, is part of our healing process.

At twelve weeks postpartum, Quinn and I completed our "fourth trimester" together and I was back to work, but I was still not yet moving freely and pain-free. By now I had been on approximately two extended walks, and on the first one I pushed myself too far and it set my healing back. The time had come to seek outside help.

When I arrived at the physical therapy office, I'm not sure what I was expecting, but not this. The exam room looked more like a visual arts major's dorm room than any medical environment I'd ever seen. A large modern jungle painting adorned the far wall, multiple rattan floor lamps cast a warm glow, and I noted the above fluorescent lights were turned off. And a corkboard tacked tall with cards and letters of all colors. When I got closer, I found they were all thank-you notes.

When the pelvic-floor therapist entered the room, she wasn't what I expected, either, with ash-blond and blue hair. She introduced herself as Blake—"or Dr. Blake, if you must"—and told me to get comfortable.

"No stirrups or speculum here," she announced as I reclined on the table after talking through my concerns. "Just a big, fluffy pillow under each leg."

During the exam, every move was precipitated by a request seeking confirmation of consent, and she not only asked this, but explained clearly to me that she would always ask first. "As the owner of a vulva," she said, "I always appreciate when doctors tell me clearly what they are going to do next."

This is what really stayed with me: How many times have I been in such exam rooms? And how many times have I been *asked* by a medical professional for my consent?

Blake made a point to leave the room and allow me to get dressed before discussing the results of my exam. When I made a joke about six weeks being for me the point at which I could walk to get the mail and that's about it, she gently stopped me.

"Your body was your partner during your daughter's birth, right?" I nodded. "And she is just as much your partner now in your healing. Let her be *with* you in this, not against you."

We both knew she was speaking beyond the scope of medical care now, woman speaking to woman. And we both knew this was wisdom.

I left her care with the sense of confidence that I had worked hard to strengthen this foundation of myself, and it showed. And I left with hope for my healing, with a plan and set of exercises to do at home to get better, as well as a plan to add another card to Blake's corkboard collection.

Over the years, I've soaked up the disregard and diminishing of doctors toward my body. I've been scoffed at for my informed care choices, and told not to worry so much when asking researched questions about the effect of past miscarriages on future pregnancies. Once as a teenager, riding alone in the ambulance after vomiting for hours due to food poisoning, I was mocked by a paramedic who made my pain his punch line, and I don't know that I've ever felt so unsafe.

But now I was soaking up the sense that my pain was heard and my body was worthy of care. I was still me, *she* was still me. Seeking the care I needed for my recovery process was a way of practicing my personhood within parenthood, as my friend Erin Lane says.

A few days later, after Quinn went down for the night, I pulled myself out of a gorgeous Epsom salt bath and felt a little light-headed (all that warmth and muscle relaxation). So I kneeled on the floor, dripping wet, head resting on my hands, to let the blood circulate. From this position, I could see my belly hanging soft and low, dripping droplets onto the soft honeycomb of my towel.

After so much stretching, straining, and exertion of strength, here was something like an encounter in that this was entirely new: an unprecedented softness. Here I was on my knees, in a posture of surrender, maybe the best place for me to be. Listening to her, being kind and gentle with my body, because she is me. We are in this together.

I will not disdain the body that harbored my daughter. I will not play vandal to the sanctuary that was and is her home.

My body tells the story of how I held space for my daughter. Why would I ever erase that from its book? This body has done tremendous things, and I would not hold it against her now that she is not as strong as I want her to be, here in the tender aftermath.

I knew then on the floor what I try to keep close to me now: I've fought the fight of my life to become this soft. No one dare ask me to give it up now—not the algorithms, the "just-pushthrough" proselytes, the "bounce back" defenders, least of all myself.

This softness, it is a hard good. But it is good.

Life stretches all of us in the way that pregnancy stretches a body. I tend to think we're all stronger than we know and that we need more gentleness than we might imagine.

Perhaps this is the gift Epiphany offers us: In the tender spaces of transition, it gives us permission to be in process. A great hope has come, and healing is still on its way. On the threshold of any beautiful beginning, we can go gently, knowing that God meets us in the very places where we most feel stretched by the now and the not yet.

10

TESSERING WELL

Easter, Again

I AM the one who makes all things new
With You in the ancient pattern of life, death, and
resurrection

What the resurrection teaches us is not how to live—but
how to live again, and again, and again!

JOHN SHEA, *The Passion and the Cross*

Spring had been rumored, and soon it was here. At first, it was just snowdrops—breaking through their rust pine needle beds, in tiny, triumphant assertions. Then the fiddlehead ferns began rising up in the garden, lush and leisurely in their stretch toward the sun. And soon you could see it out any window: green returning.

That first Easter with Quinn, we spent the weekend at my parents' house, and my dad fashioned a forsythia crown for Quinn's tiny head, which she nobly tolerated, just as he always did for me and my sisters growing up. I wore a periwinkle dress and we grilled lamb and asparagus and ate cake with candied violets my gardener sister plucked from the yard.

It was a true feast. But maybe best of all, that weekend she laughed for the first time. And this made us all laugh because it was so thrilling, and felt so fitting. Our Easter was a weekend of daffodils blooming, a dead God rising, babies laughing.

It only made us want more, and soon enough we were getting wildly undignified in service of this laugh, anything for a giggle. She found yawns hilarious, yet would not break her best poker face the second we hit "record" to capture the moment. Some experimentation offers insight: "It's the suspense that gets her," Zach says. "When she knows the best part is coming, but doesn't know quite how or when."

There's a name for this in humor theory, the study of why people laugh, known as the theory of incongruity.[1] We laugh when the actuality of events defies expectation to the point of near absurdity. We laugh when we are delighted by the surprise, the grand reversal of expectation, the "kick of the discovery."[2] In other words, a punch line is a punch line because it is a plot twist.

For babies and even for all of us, maybe that's the joke—the anticipation of joy. Maybe that's the punch line, the kicker, the thrill—knowing the best part is about to happen, and loving it already.

I can't think of anything more incongruous than life after death, and that's not even where the story begins. The Incarnation is impossibility embodied, three times over. As if it weren't impossible enough that God could be born human, as if it weren't impossible enough that God could die, God through Christ comes back to life and renders death undone. This is no slapstick, no after-hours prank; this is joy of the serious sort. The resurrection lets us in on the great joke that is nothing less than this: The way of all things under the rule of entropy is broken. Where linear time and space decree the story end in a full stop with the last breath, the resurrection rolls the stone like an ellipsis, and boldly continues the story.

The resurrection is the most unexpected, least likely coup in human history. Bishop John of Constantinople wrote, "Hell seized a body, and met God face to face. It seized earth, and encountered heaven."[3]

The story is so over the top, so beyond, the resurrection is the most belly laughable absurdity of all.

And the best part is that we've been let in on the joke. Not in the way of a cheap stunt, but in the way of the wind-in-your-hair wild freedom of a clean getaway, shouting your relief-riddled astonishment that the impossible has really just been pulled off.

No matter where you find yourself in the circle of time, no matter what your personal moment holds, the liturgical story lets us in on the end that will ultimately come. For all that has happened and all the death we have endured, all things will be made new. Resurrection will come. If I find hope in anything, I find it in this. Where death claims to have the last word, love speaks its counter through the resurrection. This is the joke. This is the joy. This is the "counter-story."[4]

And this is the consolation: In knowing the epilogue of death is life, we can find our courage to brave the bend of time's color wheel again.

The day after Quinn was born, as I was holding her in the hospital bed, a quiet came over me, and I think the most precise word for what happened next is weeping. Zach, who was with me, was alarmed, so I told him, "I'm okay. I just haven't done it yet." And I was—I wasn't sad, I just needed a *release* for all the adrenaline and cortisol that had so recently and radically drenched my nervous system. My body had gone into surge capacity in labor, and the labor was now over, but all that surging energy was still swarming inside of me, and I needed to let it out. So the tears became my release valve.

It was my body's way of completing the stress cycle, a concept that woke me up with a shock of recognition when I first read about it in Emily Nagoski and Amelia Nagoski's incredible work *Burnout*.

The authors differentiate the physiological experience of stress from the actual stressor itself, using the classic example of being chased by a lion. The lion is the stressor, but the *stress*—the heart-pumping fear and adrenaline rush—can still affect a person long after they've stopped running and are safe from threat, unless they can find a true release valve for all this tension.

The Nagoski sisters call this completing your stress cycle: giving your body a physical signal that it is safe now, the threat is past, and it is now free to release its adrenaline and be at peace. There are many ways of closing this loop, such as physical movement, which they describe as anything that moves you into your body and supports deep breathing. Other practices might be dancing it out, going for a run, allowing yourself a good cry, sharing a belly laugh or a bear hug or other means of human connection with someone you trust, or engaging in self-expression through writing, cooking, creating art, or even simply belting out your favorite song when it comes on the radio. These are all powerful signals to say, "Wow, that was real, but I'm safe now."

"Even just standing up from your chair, taking a deep breath, and tensing all your muscles for twenty seconds, then shaking it out with a big exhale, is an excellent start."[5]

If we *don't* complete the cycle, the physiological effects of stress will continue to circulate in our vital systems, locking us in a state of emergency. Of course we face stressors every day, whether lions or labor or the little catastrophes that punctuate a life, so closing our stress loops becomes an essential daily practice for our well-being.

The authors define wellness not as the static state of "perpetual safety and calm," but rather as the ability "to move fluidly from a state of adversity, risk, adventure, or excitement, back to safety and calm, and out again."[6] Well-being, in other words, does not mean you'll never be chased by lions; it just means you won't live suspended in the fear of them forever.

I think of it like the chromed thermal blankets paramedics give survivors after the crisis. The blankets are not so much for warmth or wind breaking, but offered as a physical signal to the body that *you are safe now, the lion is gone* so the heart and mind might also believe it.

If the crucifixion is the crisis of the Paschal cycle, we need a way of completing our stress cycle, even in light of the resurrection, even after the lion is gone. And in the liturgical circle, we are given this way.

In the Christian calendar, Eastertide is the fifty days following the day of resurrection. It is fifty days of feasting, a significant number in that both this period of feasting outlasts the Lenten period of fasting, and it mirrors the forty days Jesus spent with his disciples until his ascension, plus the ten additional days until Pentecost. And so we are given fifty days to absorb the astonishment of the resurrection and what this life after death means for our lives. We are given fifty days to complete our stress cycle as the Paschal cycle is completed, and we need every one of them.

After all, Holy Week is a surge capacity event. The Paschal triduum of Maundy Thursday, Good Friday, through Holy Saturday to Easter Sunday are the most high-intensity days of the entire liturgical year. These three days are a microcosm of the human experience, in their cycle of life, death, and resurrection. I have come to see Eastertide as space given for us to close the stress loops on all that has been our longest Lent, our dark Good Friday, and our silent Saturday. For all the banner days of Holy Week, Eastertide is our gateway to Ordinary Time, where most of our year and perhaps most of life itself is lived. Surely it is good to let the resurrected body signal to our bodies that we are safe now, before we carry the clench of emergency into our everyday. Surely it is good and wise to shake it off—all that high-intensity adrenaline—before entering Ordinary Time.

Completing our stress cycle is a sacred act. This is the very invitation I see pulsing at the heart of the most beautiful benediction I know, when the resurrected Christ appeared to his friends and said, "Peace be with you."

After everything, these are the four words that hold the world. Peace is the only power capable of breaking the brutal hold of fight, flight, freeze. Peace is the bear hug, the belly laugh, the huge, sweeping exhale capable of ushering our bodies from shock into divine shelter.

Only one who has experienced death can speak this peace honestly, and as such, the peace of Christ is a peace that will never overpromise, a peace we can trust with the full weight of our being. This peace is a person whose voice has cracked, whose memory holds complex trauma, and whose body bears scars, and his promise is not safety, but presence: Love is with us through the Paschal cycle, the stress cycle, the circle of time and all it might hold.

Peace be with you implies a parallel benediction: *Vigilance be released from you.* In receiving Christ's peace, we are freed to release our high-alert adrenaline and our cortisol-pumping crisis response. In the light of the resurrection, our nervous system can close its stress loop. We can let all that pent-up tension give way to the exhale of relief, and even laughter.

Here we find another humor theory, known as the theory of release. Popularized by Sigmund Freud, this theory holds that laughter is a powerful channel for "nervous energy" to be released.[7] It breaks the tension. And there is so much tension.

Listen closely: Can you hear the laughter of the holy? Easter-

tide is vibrating with the sonic joy of the Trinity, and you are invited to join the full-throated laughter of God. Yes, the scars are
real, but so are the endorphins rushing through your vital systems now as you share in the divine joke.

Frederick Buechner writes of this tension and release. He
notes that the sequence, the timing—as with any great joke—is
significant: "The worst thing isn't the last thing about the world.
It's the next to the last thing. The last thing is the best. It's the
power from on high that comes down into the world. . . . Can
you believe it? The last, best thing is the laughing deep in the
hearts of the saints, sometimes our hearts even. Yes. You are ter-
ribly loved and forgiven. Yes. You are healed. All is well."[8]

Receiving the peace and releasing the rest is what it means to
practice resurrection. And it is a practice—Easter is the gift we
will spend a lifetime living into.

Holy Week holds the highest of highs and lowest of lows on
the spectrum of human emotion. It holds shouts of hosanna, the
hope of the people, the conspiring of political powers, breaking
bread among friends, blood money, midnight prayers, the final
exhale of God as it gives way to earthquakes, and then—*and
then,* two of the most beautiful words I know—it holds stones
rolled back, death denied, the undoing of entropy.

Maybe Holy Week can be for us a space to name our lions: all
that we have endured, all the shock it has brought to our vital
systems. This is witnessed and validated by a God who suffers
with us, in the solidarity of radical empathy.

And maybe Eastertide can be for us the practice of exhale:
releasing all that has held us in high alert, so the body and soul
might indeed receive the peace of Christ.

Resurrection tells the story of the body that experienced death
and lives again. And the living Christ extends to us this very
resurrection to our bodies: *Let them live.*

I love how artist and writer Ehime Ora speaks of healing through this release: "You gotta resurrect the deep pain within you and give it a place to live that's not within your body. Let it live in art. Let it live in writing. Let it live in music. Let it be devoured by building brighter connections. Your body is not a coffin for pain to be buried in. Put it somewhere else."[9]

Make no mistake: The pain you have endured is real, but your body is not a tomb. And you are called to live. Just as Jesus called to his friend Lazarus, Jesus calls to us, "Come forth!" The peace you most long for is already yours. The shock of what you've endured must be named, but the shelter is here for you now. Eastertide calls to all of us: Rest now, and receive the peace.

The morning began like any other. Quinn was always the first to wake, her bright vocalizations bringing us hazily into a new day. Zach brought me coffee while I propped up the pillows and Quinn nursed. Slowly, slowly, we roused.

Some years ago, Zach stopped by our neighborhood bakery for coffee before work, and a grinning, mop-haired teen behind the cash register ditched the usual, forgettable pleasantries for the far more memorable "Have an auspicious day!" It's been part of our family's canon ever since, so now, most days, including this one, we bring this offbeat benediction to Quinn as part of our morning ritual. As she wiggled and we wrangled her out of jammies, we said, "Are you ready to begin Quinn's auspicious day?"

It is perhaps the prototypal benediction of parents: We just want our children to be happy. While at first this might feel like asking for everything, I have come to realize that "happy" is too small a hope for the ones we love.

Of course I want my daughter to be happy, but I also want her to be free to feel the full range of her wide and wild life. I don't want her to live bracing, suspicious of joy—a posture her parents are continually unlearning. Neither do I want her to live shrouded in denial, in the fixation of happiness at the expense of what is honest and true. Rather, I want her to feel the freedom of feeling it all, and knowing that she is not alone in any of it. So I suppose what this brings me to is that I want her to be free to live in hope—to believe that the future can be not purely ominous, but auspicious indeed.

Of course, I tend to slant toward the ominous. I have spent whole years of my life raising an eyebrow at the suggestion of bright skies ahead. And I remain suspicious of any kind of spirituality that overpromises. But if I'm taking an honest review— God being born through a birth canal, dead men walking, stardust swirling in our bones—is this not an auspicious life? I am compelled to believe that it is.

And today was particularly auspicious, as today, our daughter would become a time traveler.

I didn't necessarily plan it this way, but here's how it happened. Nine months in, four months out, and then one bright morning in April, she is reborn: back to the waters, forward into a new kind of life, in the name of the Father, Son, and Holy Spirit.

Baptism is a tesser if there ever were one.

In the waters of this sacrament, "Past and future come rushing together into the present, pouring an ocean of meaning into the little bottle of 'now,'" as N. T. Wright says.[10] Baptism is the nexus of dimensions—past, present, future; life, death, and resurrection—as we the baptized are initiated into the great belonging of the life of Christ. The water seals us into this sacred belonging, signing the promise that God is with us in all our travels and timelines, through all living, dying, and rising.

The baptismal fonts of the early church were circular in form to evoke the divine womb, reimagining in stone Jesus' invitation to be born again and the early church fathers' explicit teaching of baptism as new birth.

Historically, the baptismal font was a central part of the Easter celebration. After a lengthy catechumenate period, new believers would be baptized at the culmination of the dark night of the Easter Vigil, so they could fully participate in the Easter celebration at dawn.

The baptismal font is emblematic of the wider circle—and community through the ages—that we enter into and practice today. Like the baptismal font, sacred time is a circle—a womb that will one day release us into a reality that is re-storied by resurrection. In the meantime, we feel the long labor of this life. Living, dying, rising—these are the contractions as God labors toward our rebirth, the undercurrent of everything. This is the rhythm that remakes the world.

Through baptism, we enter the circle and become those who tesser with the movements of love. Here, at the shoreline, at the rippling edge, our tessering begins.

While our daughter, just as any child, will exercise their own free agency as they grow, for Zach and me, our imagination has always been stirred by the covenant of God as given not just to individuals but to families. This love has always been an expansive love. And like all of us, these are promises we continually live into. Baptism, to us, signifies a person's entrance to belonging, and God willing, a lifetime of becoming ahead of them. Like all births, baptism is an act of faith. It is "an identity that we spend the rest of our lives living into."[11]

So today, a few weeks after Easter, was a feast day. Our families had all come into town. The plan was pregame bagels and coffee, and a barbecue baptism after party.

For the occasion, I outfitted Quinn in a simple white sheath dress with lace bell sleeves, and an outrageous headband of flowers in blush cream and coral.

At our downtown cathedral, Quinn seemed so small in this sanctuary of vaulted stone and stained glass, and she watched everything curiously. Even with the simplicity of a private baptism, something our priest kindly offered us in the thick of pre-vaccination Covid concerns, there were more faces around her than she's ever had in her whole life. Our families and godparents gathered around the font in a circle, all masked and hand-sanitized by the gallon-sized pumps that flanked the aisles, and Reverend Amy walked us through what would happen next as part of the service.

Together we read through the baptismal liturgy in the *Book of Common Prayer*, Quinn playing with the frayed binding, ever finding the edges of a thing. When we got to the actual sprinkling part, Quinn on my hip, I asked Reverend Amy, "What do I do?"

She motioned for me to lean Quinn over the font. "Just tip her back over the brink," she said.

It was all I could do not to laugh out loud right there in the sanctuary.

Oh yes, just walk right up to the edge of everything, and lean the gravity of your tiniest beloved over the brink. Just suspend the body that is life-dependent on yours over the edge of all the terrible risks of love. What nonchalance to speak of this most existential ask. But yes, this is the very essence of baptism.

The African American spiritual "Were You There (When They Crucified My Lord)" was composed by enslaved African Americans in the nineteenth century, and it is often sung today on Good Friday in its vivid witness of suffering. The refrain leads, "Oh! Sometimes it causes me to tremble, tremble, tremble," and

I think how beautifully this expresses the gravity of the Paschal mystery and our participation in it.

Baptism is our initiation into the full-circle story of God and the Paschal mystery that pulses at its bright center. We enter the orbit the only way mortals can: trembling. And tremble we should, because this is a story in which nothing is safe and everything happens: life, death, death-defying life, trauma, transcendence, and all liminalities between.

Baptism can at times feel too bright a sacrament for the eyes to bear. After all, baptism is a birth story. To witness it is to be in the labor and delivery room—just as primal, just as intimate, just as sacred. This sacrament is just as much a water burial. I once heard the story of a seminarian who remarked, "Baptism is the coolest funeral you'll ever go to."

Baptism is both, it is everything. What a thing to witness. No wonder in the baptismal liturgy we call for the collective commitment of all who do to support any child of God going under, rising up. No wonder we renounce the devil every time.

Zach and I trembled that day before the most existential ask of parenting, as of faith itself: surrender.

I remembered the day a backyard mosquito first broke newborn skin while she was in Zach's arms, how he swore, but what I heard was the sea-frothed sorrow beneath—at the knowledge that for all the fury of his care, he could not even protect her from a fly. And now here we were being asked to entrust this little one we loved most to the waters that are both birth, burial, and sacred beginnings.

This is the Paschal mystery. Here we stood at its brink. Yet we were here because, even after everything, we believe in a love that is stronger than death. We believe in the auspicious future made possible by the resurrection.

I blinked back salt. Following Reverend Amy's direction, I

leaned our daughter back, and it felt as much a surrender as birth itself. The water poured, the oil anointed, and she took it all in with wide, curious eyes. I could see the soft spot beneath her coral flowers pulsing gently, and we stood as two exposed nerves together.

"The water will evaporate," the priest said to Zach and me, "but the oil will stay in the shape of the cross."

Then to Quinn: "You are marked as Christ's own forever."

This is what I know. Baptism is no sacrament of safeguard. These waters are no hex against harm. Sometimes this particular circle will feel like a sanctuary, a haven, a womb, and sometimes it will feel like a gladiator ring. But whatever the circle holds, there's nothing in it that can shake what will always be true: one's baptismal belonging, and the love that is with us always.

Julian of Norwich once wrote, "If there be any such lover of God on each who is continually kept [safe], I do not know of it, for it was not revealed to me. But this was revealed: that in falling and in rising we are always inestimably protected in one love."[12]

Welcome, one so loved, to the family of God.

Surely her life, surely every life, will hold a great shimmering spectrum of everything: resurrection mornings and dark nights of the soul, sweeping pandemics and paper-cut griefs, great loves, sucker punch losses, and disorienting in-betweens. For all my burning goodwill, I can't promise my daughter safe passage. But I can promise her presence in any passage.

It's when we try to press the vastness of this promise into the creviced precisions of what will and won't happen that we get into trouble. When we hinge the promise of God on outcome rather than accompaniment, we forge the signature of God into a deal God never makes. Surely this is taking God's name in vain.

When my daughter was still growing within, after the Doppler couldn't find her heartbeat and mine felt like it might stop in the waiting, my improvised desperate prayer had become, *I*

AM, With Us. In my most desperate moment I sensed what I still believe to be true: Presence is the only promise that can be made honestly before a life that holds everything.

And so to this promise we commit her: *I AM, With Her.* Through every love, loss, and liminality. Through every auspicious hour. Today, she is baptized into presence, into the life of Christ that is closer than our breath, so she will never tesser through any of it alone.

The wingspan of the human experience is wide, and it is both matched and mirrored by the far-reaching joys, pains, and in-betweens of the life of Christ as told by the liturgical narrative. This is a story that traces every contour, as if to say, *You are not crazy for feeling any of this. It's all real. And Love is with you all the way.* It mirrors our experience because it *is* our experience: the Incarnation tells the story of God entering *our* orbit, and then through baptism, ushering us into the orbit of God.

In this way, the range of the liturgical year presents itself to us as one of its greatest gifts. There is nowhere for us to go that God is not. There is no experience of love, loss, or liminality that is stranded outside of this divine witness and with-us empathy.

When we had made it safely into the second trimester after the scares of the first, my doctor had told me, "Everything looks good. You're out of the woods now."

But are we ever? There are so many woods. Life is an outright wilderness of them—dividing up the furniture with the one you thought would be your forever; gritting your teeth through the toxic work environment because you need the health insurance; grappling with the crushing weight of helplessness as the news cycle breaks your heart again and again. While it would be far preferable to live our lives where we can see the sun above the tree line, where we can feel its warmth on our skin in the safety of some gold clearing, we know the forest will always be part of the landscape.

We may not ever be out of the woods altogether, but we can live our lives in communion. We can live sealed as God's own, forever, the *I AM, With Us* in any wilderness. What's more, we are meant to.

Poet Jack Gilbert writes, "We must risk delight. We can do without pleasure, but not delight. Not enjoyment. We must have the stubbornness to accept our gladness in the ruthless furnace of this world. To make injustice the only measure of our attention is to praise the Devil."[13]

Or, as a friend once told us, "There should be champagne at Easter." Joy is the feast and it is meant to be kept.

If baptism is a birth story, then this was a birthday party.

If every baby is born looking for a face looking for them, we are reborn of the baptismal waters to the face of God and the witnessing church, who speak with one voice: *Welcome to the family of God.*

So today, we popped the corks. There was champagne, there was fifteen pounds of Zach's smoked pork barbecue with Carolina Gold sauce, pumpkin mac and cheese with fried sage and nutmeg, Little Gem lettuce heaped with smoked corn and apples, and the biggest pan of my mom's peanut butter truffle brownies I have ever seen. There was prayer and toasts and laughter, and a new kind of call-and-response for our littlest catechumen in making all things new: "Are you ready to begin Quinn's auspicious life?"

In time, Quinn does what all babies do: she grows, and every day she becomes more and more of her singular self. She launches into full-out dance every time a car with the radio on drives by.

Every dog in the neighborhood is a celebrity sighting. I will never forget the day she said "octopus," long before any child has any business voicing three-syllable words. She loves Peter Rabbit and his brass buttons, the crowd-pleasing move of busting her foot out of the high chair, and looking for the moon every night before bed.

And nothing makes her laugh like spinning does.

I set her on my hip, arms encircling her tiny frame, *ready, set* . . . and we go sailing into the wild joy of motion. I imagine she loves the way the air comes alive as if she has wings, the way the room becomes a blur of light and color, the way my hair spins out. What I love is the way she laughs with her whole body. When we stop, she says, "Again, again!" It becomes one of her first and favorite words, an encore bloomed of bliss.

For just this moment, we break the laws of gravity, we defy the empire of entropy, and we fly.

I think of us in centrifugal force, like a moon and planet in shared orbit, and the mutual thrill of being held. The gravity between us is called trust. The revolution that holds us, at our center, is called love. And the joy of this movement is in knowing it can hold our full weight. And so we spin again, laughing.

Liturgy is called the work of the people. Perhaps in its primary form, it is the work of a life.

Through the full circle of time, we tesser around and around, again and again, and we tesser well in trusting that we are held in the circumference of a love that will not let us go.

Inhabiting such a circle is humbling because it is structured so we are forever beginning again. Again, the world turns and sets the circle spinning. Here we are, singing "Silent Night" . . . again, ashes on our forehead . . . again, finding fiddleheads rising up in the garden, shouting our Easter surprise . . . again. Year after year, we begin anew.

Yet here's where it gets interesting: Year after year, we receive the invitation to go deeper in. Year after year, we find a steadiness able to sustain us through the turbulence of mortal life.

There is no such thing as "arrival," which is a myth of the linear; there is only circulation.

After all, we are circulating creatures living in a circulating universe. The world turns. The womb expands. The tides rise and fall, the moon waxes and wanes, the planets slow-dance the sky in their orbit. The body wakes and sleeps in circadian rhythm. The trees grow another ring for another year. The liturgical story cycles with the seasons, and the people of God brave its bend again. The color wheel turns and we tesser its rim. A baby is baptized, and spins with her mother. Her hair flies out.

And God is the circle "whose center is everywhere and whose circumference is nowhere."[14]

Sometimes we will experience this circulation laughing, just as sometimes it will be dizzying, and sometimes downright devastating. The world may become a blur of light and color in the best or worst of ways, but through it all, Love is the face that will never let us go, and her face shines ever toward you.

Love is the center of gravity that can steady us through any spiral. We are "radically accompanied."[15] We are held, for all the rest.

The variables are many, this is the constant. For all the centers that will not hold, this one will.

AN HONEST EPILOGUE

As any editor who makes their living shaping narratives will tell you, the only honest epilogue is an ellipsis, because the story never really ends with the last page. Every book must have its fixed borders of course, yet the narrative of a life keeps unfolding in real time, and as a reader, I always appreciate the acknowledgment of this. Just as I resist any narrative that presumes the story ends full stop with the final sentence, as if resolution is a fixed point on a flat plane, a static status, as if arrival is something that can be achieved with the right muscle and mindset.

The story always continues, and so I will not pantomime perfect closure on this one. Rather, I will end on what life offers to all of us: three small circles like stars in formation. These are mine.

When Quinn was nearly two, I took the train into New York City and I had only three intentions for this trip: (1) to spend the weekend with an old friend, (2) to eat well as only New Yorkers can, and (3) to see *Hadestown.*

I'm not the Broadway musical type, but I had heard the buzz about this one, and something in its story about singing our way through sorrow was calling my name.

"Welcome to *Hadestown,* where a song can change your fate," the ticket website told me. As I would soon learn, the narrative hangs entirely on the theme of change—the devastation of it when nothing changes, the haunting hope that everything will, the edge-of-your-seat suspense of unknowing which way fate will tilt.

The story centers on two lovers, Eurydice and Orpheus, in this reimagined Greek myth brought somehow both forward and backward into a speakeasy-throwback, postapocalyptic future. Their world is ravaged by climate change as Hades renders the earth a living hell, and yet they dare to hope things can be different.

"Come see how the world could be," Hermes, as the show's narrator, calls in the opening number, as the lights are dimmed and the story begins. Yet this invitation is double-edged, as the story reveals both a vision of a world destroyed by climate change, and a world in which true love can change everything.

It's a story that celebrates trying—trying for love, trying for liberation, trying for a better world. In a culture fixated on success stories, *Hadestown* counters with a narrative that dignifies not The Win but The Try. And all the taking heart it requires.

"It's an old song, from way back when," the opening number of *Hadestown* tells us, which is titled "The Road to Hell." And don't we all know what it's like to be walking that road. Don't we all know what it's like to watch the threat rise around us like a fever.

Like the pronunciation of Ash Wednesday, *Hadestown* tells us at the outset exactly where the story will go.

"Remember that you are dust, and to dust you shall return."

"It's a sad song," the three Fates—sashaying in their silver sequins—warn us outright.

And while we will bear the ashes, and we will bury the alleluias for a time, "We're gonna sing it again. But we're gonna sing it, anyway."

The fates weren't lying. It is a sad song. You can't help but to believe in the love story. You can't help but to be swept up in the hope of a changed world. And none of this summons the "happy ending" we all hope for, in what has to be the most unresolved ending in the history of Broadway musicals.

But then, in the final act, the stage resets, and the opening scene and song are reprised. Suddenly, after so much has happened, we're at the beginning again, and Persephone's spring has come once more in its full glory "with a love song for anyone who tries."

"We're gonna sing it again. But we're gonna sing it anyway."

It's the "anyway"—these three syllables of subversion—that brings me to tears. It's the "anyway" that brings my friend and me and the entire audience to its feet in standing ovation at the curtain call, *even though* it is a tragedy—just as we've been told—because even now, we can't help but believe their hope will be fulfilled. We can't help but believe next time it will be different.

And I am desperate for next time to be different. Because as I stand up out of my red velvet seat in the theater, applauding and blinking back whatever this is welling up in me, I am pregnant once again after another loss. I am in my first trimester where hope is both fragile and a force, and I am churning once again in the unknowing of how this story will go.

Why the "anyway"? What could possibly be worth venturing out on the road to hell again and again?

We sing because it's a love song. Because "it's a love song about someone who tries."[1]

Just like our Ash Wednesday, the show's opening and closing

"Road to Hell" is a full circle, ashes to ashes. But in between, how we sing and dance—and ours is the anthem of the "anyway." How we'll sing again and again. Because make no mistake, this life is a love song.

May we be the ones who try. May we be the ones who remember our death, and try for life anyway. May we be the ones who accept the ashes, and shout our alleluias when it's time. May we be the ones who remember we are dust, and stardust, too.

May we be the ones who take heart, who sing anyway, even after everything, knowing how deeply we are held. May we find the sacred courage to say, with the joyful trust of a child spinning, "Again" . . .

ACKNOWLEDGMENTS

British novelist Jean Rhys once wrote of writing as a lake fed by many rivers, and this work has been enriched by so many rivers.

To Zach, for seeing how this book seized me before I even knew it was a book, and whose support has sustained me through a pandemic, pregnancy loss, becoming parents, and more life than I can name here. For Handling Things so I could put down words for three years of nap times. You knew I could, I believed you, and so I did. Fourteen years and counting, you're still my favorite stranger.

To Quinn and Soren—to know you is to adore you. You have shown me whole new rooms in the house, secret gardens out back, too. It is the honor of my life to witness all you are becoming.

To Mom and Dad, for a childhood that taught me to love books and stories, love and prayers and every Thursday, so many house projects and so much sustaining pumpkin bread; your support has been the constant in the chaos. Thank you.

To Russ and Andrea, for your enduring support, watching the grands so I could edit another chapter, and the open-hearted parenting and grandparenting that have made our family what it is.

To my sisters and brothers—all my love, always. Special thanks to Allison for many weekends at our house, always bringing Pipkin and somehow endless patience with all our chaos.

To Emry, Broghan, and Daniela—our children have been so lucky to be loved by you.

I think of each of you when I say this book is here only because of you. They say writing is a solo act, but is it really?

To Lisa Jackson, my agent, for letting an early draft move you and telling me so, and for steady insights and sounding-board sessions ever since. Your wisdom has always had my trust.

To the publishing team at Convergent—Tina Constable, for joining that very first call and catching this unconventional vision; Derek Reed and Campbell Wharton, for welcoming this book to your list and supporting its way; Elizabeth Groening and Alisse Goldsmith-Wissman, for your creative energy and ideas; Craig Adams and the copyediting team, for allowing so many stets; Caroline Cunningham, for composing such a gorgeous interior; and to everyone who helped bring this book into the sacrament of print. It's been an honor to collaborate with you.

To Keren Baltzer, for being among the first to see what this book could be, and being a passionate advocate from the start. To Matt Burdette, for your depth of theological and aesthetic engagement, for at turns pushing for clarity and permitting the poetry and discerning between the two. My greatest fear was sending this manuscript to print without the rigor of meticulous edits, and thanks to you, mine did not go without. Your collective edits pushed me in every way that this editor hoped for, and always from a place of support. I receive this as a gift.

To the Very Rev. Robyn Szoke-Coolidge, for your generous offering of time and expertise in your liturgical reading, and for setting me straight where I needed it.

To Karla Colahan, the artist behind the cover design, for your powers of alchemy in taking my raw ideas and turning them into (neon!) gold. And to Dad, for bringing a resurrection fern to our house one day so we could watch it unfold from brown into living green again.

To my authors: I have learned something original from each and every one of you. Thank you for entrusting me with your words, and rest assured I have developed whole new reserves of empathy and respect for the demanding, rewarding work that you do. It is an honor every day to be in your corner and champion you on your way.

To the Slant Letter community, for being one of my all-time favorite corners of the internet. It's an honor to be in the company of such kindred creatives, and you are some of the best. Thank you for allowing me to join you in your own creative process in this way, and know that the thoughtful, courageous way you engage your writing keeps me going in mine.

To the Green Street Hooligans and best book club a girl could ask for, for every potluck, parenting real talk, hand-me-down kid clothes swaps, book recommendations, and more. Nothing gives me more hope in humanity than seeing that myth of "other people's children" busted and you bust it every day. That village people talk about? It's you.

To Natalie, Estee, Allison, Joy, Roxy, Ariana, Elissa, Shannon, Carly, and Natalia, for such generous readings of early drafts and marking them up to make this book all that it needed to be. I'm better to know each one of you and this book is better because of you. A special thanks to Estee, who knew exactly where this book wanted to begin (you were right). And to Elissa, for snagging the very first preorder, because you are the kind of friend who always brings confetti. Thank you to the Kindred Collective, for being the kind of present readers and listeners every writer hopes for, and showing me that wisdom and mischief are meant to go hand in hand.

And to you and every reader—thank you for being here. Your attentions are a gift I will never take for granted, and I hope you have found some words here worth holding close.

NOTES

CHAPTER 1: SEARCHING FOR STEADINESS

1. Janet Kalven, "Respectable Outlaw," in *The Feminine Face of God* (New York: Bantam Books, 1992), 9.
2. Gary Schmidt, *Okay for Now* (New York: Clarion Books, 2011), 224.
3. Joan Chittister, *The Liturgical Year* (Nashville, TN: Thomas Nelson, 2009), 40.

CHAPTER 2: DARING TO EXPAND

1. Oliver Burkeman, "Oliver Burkeman's Last Column: The Eight Secrets to a (Fairly) Fulfilled Life," *The Guardian*, September 4, 2020.
2. Laura Kelly Fanucci (@thismessygrace), Instagram, October 30, 2021, https://www.instagram.com/p/CVqcrZjripz/.
3. Cheryl Strayed, "Dear Sugar, the Rumpus Advice Column #64: Tiny Beautiful Things," *The Rumpus*, February 10, 2011.
4. My sister Allison famously coined this phrase, and it stuck.
5. Mandy Arioto, *Starry-Eyed: Seeing Grace in the Unfolding Constellation of Life and Motherhood* (Grand Rapids, MI: Zondervan, 2016), 160.
6. Kathryn Schulz, *Lost and Found: A Memoir*, ebook (New York: Random House, 2022).

7. Madeleine L'Engle, *The Genesis Trilogy* (Colorado Springs, CO: Shaw Books, 2001), 16.
8. Annie Dillard, *Pilgrim at Tinker Creek* (New York: HarperCollins, 2007), 36.

CHAPTER 3: NAMING THE NIGHT

1. Christy Angelle Bauman, *Theology of the Womb: Knowing God through the Body of a Woman* (Eugene, OR: Cascade Books, 2019), 67.
2. Jane Kenyon, "Taking Down the Tree," in *Collected Poems* (Minneapolis: Graywolf Press, 2005), 153.
3. W. H. Auden, "Funeral Blues," in *The Complete Works of W. H. Auden: Poems, Volume I: 1927–1939* (Princeton, NJ: Princeton University Press, 2022), 366.
4. Cole Arthur Riley, *This Here Flesh: Spirituality, Liberation, and the Stories That Make Us* (New York: Convergent, 2022), 186.
5. Amanda Held Opelt, *A Hole in the World: Finding Hope in Rituals of Grief and Healing* (Nashville, TN: Worthy Books, 2022), 219.
6. Tish Harrison Warren, *Prayer in the Night* (Carol Stream, IL: InterVarsity, 2021), 15.
7. D. H. Lawrence, *Lady Chatterley's Lover* (New York: Random House, 1983), 362.

CHAPTER 4: REDEFINING RESILIENCE

1. "Paschal," meaning the Holy Week sequence of Christ's life, death, and resurrection, which happened historically during the Hebrew Passover.
2. Library of America. Review of *A Wrinkle in Time* by Madeleine L'Engle. "The Kairos Novels (Boxed Set)—Library of America," December 7, 2023. https://www.loa.org/books/584-the-kairos-novels-boxed-set/.
3. Madeleine L'Engle, *A Wrinkle in Time* (New York: Square Fish, 2012), 75.
4. While I find consolation in this description of a time for everything, I am unsettled by its seeming suggestion that there is ever a time for the violences of hate and war. Even this is a text to wrangle with, and I do not wish to misrepresent or oversimplify this.
5. Parker Palmer, *Let Your Life Speak* (San Francisco: Jossey-Bass, 2000), 98.

CHAPTER 5: REMEMBERING YOUR DEATH, TRYING FOR LIFE

1. Sister Theresa Aletheia Noble, *Remember Your Death: Memento Mori Lenten Devotional,* ebook (Boston: Pauline Press, 2019).
2. Seth Haines, *The Book of Waking Up,* ebook (Grand Rapids, MI: Zondervan, 2020).
3. Nadia Bolz-Weber, *Accidental Saints: Finding God in All the Wrong People* (New York: Convergent Books, 2015), 113.
4. Esprit Smith, "5 Things to Know about NASA's New Mineral Dust Detector," NASA, June 6, 2022, https://climate.nasa.gov/news/3183/5 -things-to-know-about-nasas-new-mineral-dust-detector/.
5. Ernest Becker, *The Denial of Death* (New York: Free Press, 2007), 96.
6. Carl Sagan, *Cosmos,* PBS.
7. Elizabeth Howell, "Humans Really Are Made of Stardust, and a New Study Proves It," *Space,* January 10, 2017.
8. Wendell Berry, *The Unsettling of America: Culture and Agriculture* (Berkeley, CA: Counterpoint Press, 2015), 86.
9. Jan Richardson, "Ash Wednesday: The Terrible, Marvelous Dust," *The Painted Prayerbook,* February 13, 2015, https://paintedprayerbook.com/ 2015/02/13/ash-wednesday-the-terrible-marvelous-dust/.
10. Martie Haselton, *Hormonal* (New York: Little, Brown and Company, 2018), 16.
11. "Menstrual Cycles as a Fifth Vital Sign," US Department of Health and Human Services, last reviewed September 13, 2021, https://www.nichd .nih.gov/about/org/od/directors_corner/prev_updates/menstrual -cycles#.
12. Charles Taylor, *A Secular Age* (Cambridge, MA: Harvard University Press, 2007), 771.
13. The term "cycle syncing" was popularized by Alisa Vitti, an integrative nutritionist and women's hormone expert, in her debut book *Woman Code,* published in 2014.
14. The menstrual cycle is just one of the cycles people experience, and if this particular cycle does not resonate with your experience, other rich cyclical metaphors include the natural seasons or the lunar cycle. I will focus on the menstrual cycle in this chapter because it is one of the most overlooked and understudied, as reflective of the ways women's experiences are so often marginalized in modern healthcare.
15. If any of this sniffs of too "woo-woo" to you, I would gently suggest that this reaction is a holdover of the wide effects of marginalization of wom-

en's experiences in healthcare. How can the biological experience of half the earth's population be a fringe conversation—and yet, it is.

16. Katarzyna Galasinska and Aleksandra Szymkow, "The More Fertile, the More Creative: Changes in Women's Creative Potential Across the Ovulatory Cycle," *International Journal of Environmental Research and Public Health* (May 18, 2021): 5390, https://www.ncbi.nlm.nih.gov/pmc/articles/PMC8158362/.

17. Lara Schleifenbaum et al., "Women Feel More Attractive Before Ovulation: Evidence from a Large-scale Online Diary Study," *Evolutionary Human Sciences* 3 (2021): e47, https://www.ncbi.nlm.nih.gov/pmc/articles/PMC10427307/.

18. Alisa Vitti, "The Menstrual Phase: Support Your Body with the Cycle Syncing Method," *Flo Living,* last updated June 16, 2023, https://www.floliving.com/menstrual-phase/.

19. Katherine May, *Wintering* (New York: Riverhead Books, 2020), 11.

20. Alisa Vitti, *Flo Living,* https://floliving.com/blog/cycle-syncing-explained.

21. Anastasia Berg, "Now Is as Good a Time as Any to Start a Family," *The New York Times,* April 30, 2020.

22. Billy-Ray Belcourt, *A History of My Brief Body,* ebook (Columbus, OH: Two Dollar Radio, 2020).

23. Madeleine L'Engle, *Bright Evening Star* (New York: Crown Publishing Group, 2018), 196.

24. Alexander Schmemann, *Great Lent: Journey to Pascha,* ebook (Yonkers, NY: St Vladimir's Seminary Press, 1969).

CHAPTER 6: RECEIVING THE JOY

1. Mike Gray, "Ready, Steady . . . Kook!" *Q Magazine,* May 1998, https://thedent.com/q0598.html.

2. Philip Pfatteicher, *Journey into the Heart of God* (New York: Oxford University Press, 2013), 217.

3. Joan Chittister, *The Liturgical Year* (Nashville, TN: Thomas Nelson, 2009), 160.

4. Brené Brown, *Atlas of the Heart* (New York: Random House, 2021), 216.

5. Elizabeth Dias, "The Last Anointing," *The New York Times,* June 6, 2020, https://www.nytimes.com/interactive/2020/06/06/us/coronavirus-priests-last-rites.html.

6. Elizabeth Dias and Audra D. S. Burch, "Our 'Before' No Longer Makes Sense. How Do We Live Now?," *The New York Times,* April 5, 2021,

https://www.nytimes.com/interactive/2021/04/05/us/coronavirus
-pandemic.html.

7. Sinéad Gleeson, *Constellations*, ebook (New York: Mariner Books, 2019).
8. Jana Marguerite Bennett, *Water Is Thicker Than Blood* (New York: Oxford University Press, 2008), 44.

CHAPTER 7: STAYING WITH YOUR BREATH

1. Hillary McBride, *The Wisdom of Your Body* (Grand Rapids, MI: Brazos Press, 2021), 223.
2. Rabbi Arthur Waskow, *Dancing in God's Earthquake* (Maryknoll, NY: Orbis Books, 2020), xxxii.
3. Arthur Waskow, "I Can't Breathe, We Can't Breathe, Earth Can't Breathe," The Open Siddur Project, July 27, 2020, https://opensiddur .org/prayers/collective-welfare/trouble/ecotastrophes/i-cant-breathe-we -cant-breathe-earth-cant-breathe-a-prayer-poem-by-rabbi-arthur -waskow-the-shalom-center-2020/.
4. Mary Oliver, *West Wind: Poems and Prose Poems* (New York: Houghton Mifflin, 1997), 62.
5. Louise Erdrich, *The Blue Jay's Dance* (New York: Harper Perennial, 2010), 12.
6. Dr. Nicole Calloway Rankins, "Episode 57: Using the Bloom Method to Prepare Physically for Birth and Postpartum Healing with Brooke Cates," *All About Pregnancy and Birth Podcast*, accessed January 15, 2022, https://drnicolerankins.com/episode57/#transcript.
7. Attributed to Viktor Frankl.
8. Rabbi Dennis S. Ross, *A Year with Martin Buber* (Lincoln, NE: Jewish Publication Society, 2021), xix.
9. Jon Kabat-Zinn, *Full Catastrophe Living* (New York: Bantam Dell, 2005), 6.
10. Lucinda Williams, *Down Where the Spirit Meets the Bone*, Highway 20 Records, 2014, music album.
11. Osheta Moore, *Shalom Sistas* (Harrisonburg, VA: Herald Press, 2017), 31.
12. Dorris Walker-Taylor, interview with Amy Julia Becker, *Reimagining the Good Life*, podcast audio, March 9, 2021, https://www.buzzsprout.com/ 719016/8099134.
13. Shauna Niequist, *Present over Perfect* (Grand Rapids, MI: Zondervan, 2016), 145.

CHAPTER 8: PRACTICING INCARNATION

1. Fleming Rutledge, *Advent* (Grand Rapids, MI: Eerdmans Publishing Co., 2018), 251.
2. Ibid., 7.
3. Nancy Shute, "Beyond Birth: A Child's Cells May Help or Harm the Mother Long after Delivery," *Scientific American,* April 30, 2010.
4. William F. N. Chan et al., "Male Microchimerism in the Human Female Brain," *PLOS ONE* (2012), https://doi.org/10.1371/journal.pone.0045592.
5. "Living into the Tension of Advent: Cole Arthur Riley," The Allender Center, December 11, 2020, https://theallendercenter.org/2020/12/living-tension-advent-cole-arthur-riley/.
6. F. Gary Cunningham et al., eds., "Maternal Physiology," chap. 4 in *Williams Obstetrics,* 25th ed. (New York: McGraw Hill, 2018), https://obgyn.mhmedical.com/content.aspx?bookid=1918&sectionid=144754618.
7. Diana Spalding et al., *The Motherly Guide to Becoming Mama* (Boulder, CO: Sounds True, 2020), 345.
8. Quoted in Elizabeth Johnson, *She Who Is* (New York: Crossroad Publishing, 2017), 101.
9. Phyllis Trible, *God and the Rhetoric of Sexuality* (Philadelphia: Fortress Press, 1978), 33.
10. Remy Tumin et al., "Coronavirus Surge, Georgia, Candice Bergen: Your Weekend Briefing," *The New York Times,* December 6, 2020.
11. Louise Erdrich, *The Blue Jay's Dance* (New York: Harper Perennial, 2010), 41.
12. Erdrich, *The Blue Jay's Dance,* 44.
13. Curt Thompson, *The Soul of Shame* (Downers Grove, IL: InterVarsity Press, 2015), 138.
14. Kamand Kojouri, quoted in Diana Butler Bass, "December 20: Advent Calendar," *The Cottage,* December 20, 2021, https://dianabutlerbass.substack.com/p/december-20-advent-calendar.
15. Johnson, *She Who Is* (New York: Crossroad Publishing, 1992), 101.

CHAPTER 9: GOING GENTLY INTO THE NEW

1. Sinéad Gleeson, *Constellations,* ebook (New York: Houghton Mifflin Harcourt, 2019).
2. Angela Garbes, *Like a Mother* (New York: HarperCollins, 2018), 144.

3. Meaghan O'Connell, *And Now We Have Everything* (New York: Back Bay Books, 2019), 115.
4. Rufi Thorpe, "Mother, Writer, Monster, Maid," *VELA*, accessed December 9, 2023.
5. Carla Bruce-Eddings, "I Found a New Appreciation for My Body," *The New York Times*, May 5, 2020, https://www.nytimes.com/interactive/2020/05/05/parenting/how-motherhood-changed-us.html#body_image.
6. Shauna Niequist (@sniequist), X, February 15, 2015, 9:51 a.m., https://twitter.com/sniequist/status/1096421859199987714.
7. *Britannica*, s.v. "amen," accessed December 9, 2023, https://www.britannica.com/topic/amen-prayer.
8. Nancy Eiesland, *The Disabled God: Toward a Liberatory Theology of Disability* (Nashville: Abingdon, 1994), 100.
9. K. J. Ramsey, "You Are More than You Can See," *Embodied*, September 2, 2023, https://kjramseywrites.substack.com/p/you-are-more-than-you-can-see.

CHAPTER 10: TESSERING WELL

1. Giovanni Sabato, "What's So Funny? The Science of Why We Laugh," *Scientific American*, June 26, 2019.
2. Richard Feynman, *The Pleasure of Finding Things Out* (New York: Basic Books, 1999), 26.
3. Bishop John of Constantinople, "Death, Where Is Your Sting," quoted in Philip Pfatteicher, *Journey into the Heart of God* (New York: Oxford University Press, 2013), 223.
4. Osheta Moore, *Shalom Sistas* (Harrisonburg, VA: Herald Press, 2017), 31.
5. Emily Nagoski et al., *Burnout: The Secret to Unlocking the Stress Cycle* (New York: Ballantine Books, 2019), 15.
6. Nagoski, *Burnout*, 27.
7. Sabato, "What's So Funny?"
8. Frederick Buechner, *The Final Beast* (New York: Atheneum, 1965), 175.
9. Ehime Ora (@ehimeora), X, October 17, 2021, 12:51 a.m., https://twitter.com/ehimeora/status/1449598868841279488.
10. N. T. Wright, *The Meal Jesus Gave Us: Understanding Holy Communion*, rev. ed. (Louisville, KY: Westminster John Knox Press, 2015), 51.
11. James V. Brownson, *The Promise of Baptism* (Grand Rapids, MI: Eerdmans Publishing Co., 2007), 52.

12. Julian of Norwich, *Revelations of Divine Love*. Translated by Barry Windeatt (Oxford: Oxford University Press, 2015), 161.
13. Jack Gilbert, *Refusing Heaven* (New York: Alfred A. Knopf, 2005), 3.
14. Trismegistus, *Miscellaneous Notes,* 3, in Christy Angelle Bauman, *Theology of the Womb: Knowing God through the Body of a Woman* (Eugene, OR: Cascade Books, 2019), 122.
15. Wendy Wright, *The Vigil* (Nashville, TN: Upper Room, 1992), 105.

AN HONEST EPILOGUE

1. Anaïs Mitchell, "The Road to Hell," *Hadestown* (Original Broadway Cast Recording), Sing It Again Records, 2019.

ABOUT THE AUTHOR

STEPHANIE DUNCAN SMITH is an executive editor who develops award-winning and best-selling authors at Baker Books, and previously at HarperCollins. She is the creator of Slant Letter, a popular Substack email newsletter for writers looking to deepen their craft and do it in style. Duncan Smith completed her master's in theology at Western Theological Seminary, where she was the winner of the Frederick Buechner Prize for Excellence in Writing. She lives with her husband, Zach, a professor, and their two children in Harrisburg, Pennsylvania.

slantletter.com
Instagram: @stephduncansmith